Games from
Childhood Past

About the Author

Caroline Goodfellow was the Curator of Dolls and Toys for the Victoria and Albert Museum, London. She has written a number of books and articles on dolls and games and continues to lecture on these subjects as well as being an expert advisor for television and radio programmes. She is a member of Board Games Studies, an international society of experts studying board games.

Games from Childhood Past

Cats Cradle, Hide and Seek and the Royal Game of Ur

Caroline Goodfellow

First published 2008
This paperback edition first published 2023

The History Press
97 St George's Place, Cheltenham,
Gloucestershire, GL50 3QB
www.thehistorypress.co.uk

British Library Cataloguing in Publication Data.
A catalogue record for this book is available from the British Library.

ISBN 978 1 80399 534 2

Typesetting and origination by The History Press
Printed and bound in Great Britain by TJ Books Limited, Padstow, Cornwall.

Trees for LYfe

Contents

List of Illustrations

10   *Whipping Top*. Illustrated on a child's pewter dish that has letters of the alphabet around the outer edge. American, 1890–1910

11   *Hobby Horse* ((SIC) Designer Services.com/John Williams, © 2007)

12   *Diabolo* ((SIC) Designer Services.com/John Williams, © 2007)

13   Playing a game of marbles. Illustration from *Wonderland of Work*, published by Cassell, Petter, Galpin & Co., about 1880

14   Young women playing *Knucklebones*. Made of terracotta; said to be have been from Capua and made in Campania or Puglia, southern Italy; Hellenistic Greek, 330–300 BC (© The Trustees of the British Museum)

15   *Stilts* ((SIC) Designer Services.com/John Williams, © 2007)

16   Flying a kite ((SIC) Designer Services.com/John Williams, © 2007)

17   *Piñata* ((SIC) Designer Services.com/John Williams, © 2007)

18   *Solitaire* board. Turned wood and glass marbles, English, 2004.

19   *Tangram*. Polished wood. (© Design Master Associates, Made in China, 2005)

20   *Giant Dominoes*. Hand-finished wood; designed by Justine Cardy and made by Garden Games Limited; English, 2004. (© Garden Games Limited, 2004)

21   *Noughts and Crosses*. Wood, designed and made by Jaques & Co. Ltd, 2006. (© Jaques & Co. Ltd)

22   *Nine Men's Morris*. Polished and stained wood, made by James Masters. (© James Masters, English, 2006)

23   *Giant Connect 4*. Plastic, designed by Justine Cardy and made by Garden Games Ltd, English, 2005. A large-scale wooden version of the game *BIG 4* is also available but it is more suitable for indoor use. (© Garden Games Ltd)

37 *Go*. Close-up of the board showing the placement of the pieces on the lines and not within the squares (© James Masters)

38 *Il Gioco Dell'oca. DILET = TEVOLE per chi gioco e chi non gioco* (The Pleasing Game of Goose) Si Vendono Grana 5 Presso A Rosso a S Biaso n. 107. Published in Italy about 1750. (© Victoria and Albert Museum)

39 *Nouveau Jeu de L'oie*.[1] Hand-coloured engraving mounted on card, French, about 1850.[2]

40 *The New and Favourite Game of Mother Goose and the Golden Egg*.[3] Published and sold wholesale by, John Wallis Sr, 13 Warwick Square and retail by John Wallis Jr, 188 The Strand, London, 13 November 1808. (©Victoria and Albert Museum)

41 *Dice*. Made of pewter in the style of dice hammered from lead musket balls by soldiers in the field so they may play dice games. American, 2006. (© Cooperman Company)

42 *A New Royal Geographical Pastime for England and Wales*. 'Whereby the Distance of each Town is laid down from London in measured miles being a very amusing game to play with a teetotum, ivory pillars and counters.' Published by Robert Sayer, No. 53 Fleet Street, London, 1 June 1787. (© Victoria and Albert Museum)

43 *The Panorama of Europe, A New Game*. Published by J. & E. Wallis, 42 Skinner Street, London and I. Wallis Jr. Marine Library, Sidmouth, Devon, 1 November 1815. (© Victoria and Albert Museum)

44 *Walker's New Geographical Game Exhibiting a Tour Through Europe*. Published for the author and sold by W. & T. Darton, Holborn Hill, London, 1 May 1810. (© Victoria and Albert Museum)

45 *A Tour Through the British Colonies and Foreign Possessions and Dioramic Game of the Overland Route to India*. Published by The Historical Games Company as a

54   Die, markers and counters. Issued with the new game
      and made of plastic representing bone.

55   *La Vie Humaine, Un Nouveau Jeu*. Printed on silk and
      published by Simon Schropp; German, about 1800.
      (© Victoria and Albert Museum)

56   Laurie and Whittle's *New Moral and Entertaining Game
      of The Mansion Of Happiness*[4] subtitled *Virtue Rewarded
      and Vice Punished Published* by Robert Laurie and James
      Whittle, 53 Fleet Street, London, 13 October 1800.
      (© Victoria and Albert Museum)

57   *Every Man to His Station*. Published by The Historical
      Games Company as a replica of the original game,
      English, 1994. (© Victoria and Albert Museum)

58   *Snakes and Ladders*. ((SIC) Designer Services.com/John
      Williams, © 2007)

59   *Pachisi*. Various woods and cowrie shells, made by James
      Masters, English, 2006 (© James Masters)

60   *Ludo*. Wood, stained and painted, made by James
      Masters, English, 2006. (© James Masters)

61   *Monopoly*.[5] Manufactured and distributed by
      Waddington Games Ltd, England. (© 1993 Tonka
      Corporation)

62   *Cluedo*. Printed and made in England by Waddington
      Games Ltd (© 1975 Waddington Games Ltd)

63   *221B Baker Street*, The Master Detective Game.
      Published by H.P. Gibson & Sons Ltd (© Jay Moriarty,
      1975)

64   *The Grosvenor Series*. Published *c*. 1920 by Charles & Son

65   *Boggle*. Tonka Corporation © 1992

66   *Pictionary*. Published by Parker Games. (© 1987)

67   *Totally Dingbats*. Published by Waddingtons Games Ltd,
      1990/1992. Game devised by Paul Sellers. Dingbats ®
      is a registered trade mark of Paul Sellers, for the game
      manufactured and sold under exclusive licence to
      Waddingtons Games Ltd.

Introduction

Games are played for enjoyment, as a way to actively pass the time. For some they are a method of relaxation and for others, ways to compete without the rivalry of serious business. Yet for others they are a method of testing the abilities of one's opponents, and for some complete time wasting.

The age of the player does determine the games played, however, the same game may be played by people of different ages. Physical and mental development does have some bearing on the games. For example, *Chess* is unlikely to be the game of a one-year-old child whereas such a child would be happy playing *Pat-a-Cake, Pat-a-Cake*. Likewise, most children between the ages of five and twelve will enjoy running and jumping games as well as board games such as *Chess*. Families may play games together with the different ages equally sharing the enjoyment games present with older children and adults helping younger people with some of the more intricate or subtle rules. Some games seem to be adult only ones but when one considers that many of the board games developed in the eighteenth century were designed for children under the age of twelve the dividing lines become very blurred.

Some games have such long histories that it is not possible to assign particular age groups to them. However, illustrations do exist showing games being played. Egyptian wall paintings show pharaohs musing over their next move. Game boards have been found cut into stones between seats in Roman amphitheatres, which suggest that people played games while waiting for main events to be staged. Even today, men, women and children will be found playing board games in parks and cafés on formal boards or even on hastily cut boards dug into the ground. Many games cross the language divide too. People will often sit down at a game board in a strange country, start to play and attempt to converse while doing so.

Primarily this book is about children's games. Those games played by children for their own amusement. The crossover between whether a game is for a child or an adult is very indistinct, with all ages lending its own weight to any particular activity. Running, skipping and jumping are very normal activities for young children but they are transformed into skilled Olympic feats for adults. These were the basic games of the original Olympic Games held in Greece. The games test the strength and agility of the competitors not dissimilar to the children running about in a park. They too are testing their own strength and agility.

Games are competitive, be they against oneself as in *Solitaire* or *Hop Scotch*, or against others. Physical games and board games for only two players are very competitive. Two players are pitting their abilities against each other, usually attempting to outwit each other or tempting the opponent to make a mistake. In fact, many board games for two players are referred to as Games of Strategy. As the number of players in a game increases, the competitiveness decreases. Many games for more than two rely on chance, the roll of dice and the spin of a teetotum or the turn of a card. Likewise, *Tag* with lots of players is easier than a running game with only two. All such games tend to be less serious, often more noisy and usually of a shorter duration than games for only one or two players.

Although the avid games player will take his game very seriously, the same game may be played just for fun but in both cases, the people involved are playing for enjoyment. It can be very difficult if one player is taking his game seriously while the others are not, this in its extreme can lead to arguments. Arguments may also occur when players are so competitive that they resent others winning. Cheating is also a good basis for arguments and it may result in players leaving a game with the statement, 'If you are going to cheat I am not playing with you ever again.' This rarely means what is says, it just means until the next time but beware.

Although some games are referred to in the book, they are not actively described. Games such as *Chess* and *Backgammon* are well documented and there are many books describing how to play them. This book describes some very well-known games as well as some more obscure ones. All were or are played by children or within the confines of a family. This is not to say that the games are never played with by older children or adults. Sometimes, a game designed for children is more often played and enjoyed by adults. Many modern games and a few much older ones are now played as international tournaments. Quite a number have been modified so they may be played on the Internet and others as computer games.

As the book was being researched, many new suggestions for games were added. By talking about the book, it triggered memories of childhood activities often with side comments such as, 'I was so bad at skipping and hopping, I remember it seemed to become my job to turn the ropes.' One of the most memorable occasions was a group dining out who recalled playing *Pass the Button*; they then made a game of it around the table. Like the games, this book should be enjoyed; it may even bring back happy memories.

So sit back and let play begin!

Games with Little or No Equipment

Anywhere there are children, they will be skipping or running, playing with a ball, or walking backwards. This is not restricted to school playgrounds or organised events, children use their bodies to express themselves, to show the sheer exuberance of being young and fit. Handstands, cartwheels and wheelbarrow races, intricate step movements and rolling on the ground are some of but many games children will play by themselves and with others without adult supervision.

One child or many children in any open space may play such games. At one time, children moved freely around their neighbourhoods, played in the parks, fields, school grounds and even in the streets. Sadly, many areas in the developed world are now restricted through health and safety or traffic. Parents and school authorities are often worried that their children will be harmed by games they themselves played. However, many adults do not see what the children get up to when by themselves; they will organise tag games and running games and play conkers.

Some games require an object to facilitate play and there is always a crossover between playing a game and playing with a toy. The simplest, or arguably the most complex, are games without equipment or formal rules. Many of these games formed the basis of the original Olympic Games which represented feats of skill and endurance.

Running Around

Running around is a real child characteristic, particularly for those under fourteen. It may be a simple chase between two, a well defined game of *Tag* or perhaps a run with a start and finish point.

The most common game is *Tag*. Found throughout the world, it has many names such as *It*, or *Catch as Catch Can*. This is a simple game requiring more than two people, with energy and imagination. The players divide with one person being the chaser or IT, and the rest being chased. The aim is for the single player to catch one of the others, so that the caught player becomes the IT. With the cooperation of all the players, games with more sophistication can be played. There are many variations and these are but a few of the well-known universal games.

Hide and Seek is the best known variation of *Tag*. The chaser must turn his back on the others, count as quickly as possible to a set number, usually 100, while the others attempt to hide. When the counting has finished the usual statement is, 'Ready or not I am coming.' The player turns, locates the others and chases around while attempting to catch one player from the group.

Some games bear simple names reflecting the activity. For example, the players may decide that some items may be deemed *Safe Spots*, such as trees if in a park, so any chased player is safe if he is touching one. *Hold the Spot* requires a player who has been caught to hold that part of his body that was touched by the chasing player. If it is a sunny day, a player may be caught if the chaser steps on his shadow, thus *Shadow Tag*.

Line Tag has lines of players, each holding the hand of the one in front, attempting to block the chasing player from attaching himself to the end of a line. Should he do so, the player at the front of the line becomes the chaser.

In *Follow my Leader*, the players form a circle by joining hands, with the IT inside and the player being chased outside. The chased player may go in and out of the circle, the others allowing him to do so by raising their hands and the IT must follow exactly or forfeit the game. When tagged, the player returns to the circle, the IT becomes the chased one and a player from the circle is chosen to be IT. A similar game of *Cat and Mouse* may be played where the cat inside the circle attempts to escape to catch the mouse. In this game, the hands are not linked but the players may use their bodies as blocks.

Another circle and blocking game, sometimes called *Fox and Rabbits*, can be played when there several children from which one is chosen to be the rabbit and one the fox. The rest of the group divide and link hands to form warrens, each with a resident rabbit, in which the chased rabbit may hide. The aim of the fox is to catch the rabbit, which may enter any of the warrens but in doing do displaces the resident rabbit who then must evade the fox. Once the fox catches a rabbit, he joins one of the warrens and the caught rabbit becomes the fox.

Blind Man's Bluff also requires a circle but less running about. The chaser within the circle wears a blindfold and his aim is to chase another player. However, there are some rules to give him an advantage. Initially the players move round and when he says stop, he points and the player who is pointed at must move into the circle. If this player is caught, the chaser must identify him either by feeling his face or by asking questions. If successful, the chaser retires to join the circle.

All these variations require the group to play as a unit, all know the rules and yet there are no formal rules. Children of all cultures play these games and while there are many variations, the games of *Tag* are still ones of running and chasing and being chased.

Racing Games

Racing games are more formal than the *Tag* games as they have a start and finish point. Running in a straight line is the simplest but there are many variations, which bring skill as well as talent into the equation. To introduce a challenge to any race, these are a few of the changes players can make.

Three-Legged Racing with a partner requires much cooperation and coordination between the runners. One leg of each player is tied to his partner's and together they must run the race as a unit. Not an easy exercise, which often results in laughter as the runners fall, get up and fall again. A variation of the game that is a combination with the *Sack Race* is to tie the legs of each runner together at the knee forcing them to hobble along rather than run or hop the race.

The *Sack Race* needs balance, speed and the ability to hop. The players are each in a sack or pillowcase, which they themselves must hold up. They travel the course hopping rather than running. Again, usually there are tumbles as feet are caught in the sacks thus overbalancing the child.

Follow My Leader, a slight variation on the game *Simon Says*, requires the runners to follow a variety of movements governed by a chosen leader. If he runs, the rest run, if he hops, the rest hop and so on. Anyone unable to follow drops out and the winner is the one who remains at the end. Many decide a time limit on this game otherwise the same person tends always to be the leader.

Egg and Spoon Race is often a more organised party game, as the eggs need to be hard boiled; however, it is a good race game where the winner is the first person to finish with his egg and spoon intact. Sometimes cheating is involved, usually holding on to the egg, but again it is a laughter run.

The game *Musical Chairs* requires the cooperation of an outsider, often a parent or older child who supervises the music. A group of chairs numbering one less than the number of children is placed in a circle. While the music plays the children run around the chairs and when the music stops they must gain a seat. The child who does not sit down leaves the game and a chair is removed. It is played until only one chair and two children remain and the child who sits on this last chair is the winner.

Relay Races are formally arranged with two or more groups competing to win. When seen in the Olympic Games there is a baton passed between the runners; however, in the less formal arrangements of a school or children simply enjoying this game, the runners tap the next people to run. This type of race may be augmented by having a goal at each lap such as carrying a spoonful of water to a receptacle while running, the winners being the ones who transport the most water in the quickest time.

And finally, the all-time favourite with a song to match is *Oranges and Lemons*. Two players, one the orange and the other the lemon, form an arch through which all the others must run. As the song reaches its end with the words 'Chop! Chop! Chop!', the 'arch' collapses trapping one of the runners. He must say either orange or lemon and replace the appropriate player forming the arch. As with many other games, this one reflects a period of brutality in London. Other such games are *Mary, Mary Quite Contrary* and *London Bridge is Falling Down*. This is not restricted to England; many European events are retold as children's games, often with nursery rhymes to accompany them.

Hopping, Skipping and Jumping

Not all games require so much running around. There are hopping games such as *Hop Scotch* and *Leap Frog*, skipping games with one or two ropes and quieter games such as *Conkers* and *Pass the Parcel*.

The traditional game of *Hop Scotch* is played around the world. It requires a grid, marked out with chalk on a pavement or scratched into earth. Some school grounds have the design permanently painted on the tarmac. The grid may have as many as twelve or fifteen spaces, be a square, oblong or spiral. A counter is thrown onto the grid, sometimes square by square, and the child hops to that space, picks up the counter and tosses it forward again. The aim of the game is to throw and hop both up and down the grid without either the counter or the player's foot touching a line. Variations include hopping with both feet together and hopping on alternate feet at each throw. Children often make their own rules for the game and, of course, it is a game that may be played by one child alone.

A rather aggressive hopping game, not encouraged now, had a number of different names but in England, it was called *Cock Fighting*. The players held on to one foot and hopped while attempting to push each other off balance so the opponent drops his foot or put his foot to the ground.

Leap Frog, on the other hand, needs more than one person. In recent years, however, cities and towns have provided ideal objects to be leapt in the form of bollards. These a child may leap instead of walking around often down the whole length of a road. In the original game, one child bends over to form an obstacle over which a second child leaps by placing his hands on the first child's back. He then in turn bends over while the second child leaps. If there are more children, they can form teams and make the game into a race.

Skipping may be a simple step, somewhere between running and hopping or it might be hopping over puddles, sticks and other items found on the ground. However, skipping games tend to be augmented with a rope. It may be a rope about four feet long held by the skipper, or a much longer one held by two people for a third or more persons to skip. This may also become a set of two ropes, turned alternately for the more practised skipper. This is often referred to as *Double Dutch Skipping*. Skipping with ropes needs practice and some dexterity. It is also a favourite exercise form for boxers to maintain their agility.

A slight variation, especially if there are a number of children, is a game of *Rope Skipping* or *Jumping*. One child holds the rope quite close to the ground and spins it around for the others to jump over. It usually results in much pushing and shoving. The last child to remain standing is the winner and has the rather dubious pleasure of becoming the spinner.

One of the most popular running, skipping and jumping games, played for many centuries, has completely disappeared from most developed countries in the last fifty years – the *Whipping Hoop*. A small stick was used to propel a large hoop along the ground. A child could play with this toy by itself or with his friends. In the 1950s, the hoop was turned into the *Hula Hoop*. Said to have been based on seeing Australian children swinging bamboo hoops, Wham-O-Toys issued plastic hoops made from petroleum by-products in 1957. Swung around the body and kept up by moving and swaying the body the player aimed at the greatest number of turns of the hoop before it fell down.

Whipping Tops is a similar game to the *Hoop* but not as active, there is no running involved. The top is set spinning and kept spinning by 'whipping' it with a small stick or piece of leather.

A child sitting astride a stick, hopping and running in imitation of riding a horse is an old game, thought to have been played in Greek and Roman times. The *Hobby Horse* represents cowboys and indians, knights on horseback and warrior princes. On your own or with a group, games of all kinds could be played limited only by one's imagination.

Less Running, Skipping and Jumping

Not all games require huge amounts of effort. Some require dexterity and agility. As with the more energetic games, most have been known for hundreds of years and are played all over the world by many different cultures.

The *Yo-Yo*, featured on a Greek vase, is still a favourite game requiring a fair degree of ability to keep the disc spinning. It is merely a slit disc tied to a length of string. As a player becomes more skilled, he may perform 'tricks' making the movement of the yo-yo a significant part of the exhibition. International competitions take place and it is often adults rather than children who enjoy the play.

Similarly, *Cat's Cradle* may be played by all ages. A simple knotted length of string and a few hand movements create a web of patterns. This game was a particular favourite with the Inuit people of the Arctic long before Europeans explored the region. It may be because during some months each year it was impossible to be outside to exercise. There are also tales that it could only be played by girls or women as the string was too intricate for the male hand. However, some of the greatest exponents of the game are men.

Cup and Ball or *Bilboquet* is another international game now played by everyone. Eye and hand coordination skills are needed to catch a ball in a stick end. More recently in England, a like game was the *Biff Bat*, a table tennis bat with a small rubber ball attached by a length of elastic. The game was to count the number of times the ball could be hit before being missed.

Not seen in England for some years now but still a firm favourite in China is the *Diabolo* – a double cone shaped block played on a string between two handles. Thought to have been introduced into Europe from China in the eighteenth century, the aim is to keep the diabolo on the string while it spins and moves along it. Accomplished players and professionals such as jugglers will toss the diabolo and catch it again or perhaps pass it to another player.

Less skill but patience and dexterity are need for *Spillikins* or *Pick Up Sticks*. During the nineteenth century, manufactured sets of this game were made; however, it needs only a group of similar sticks, matches or toothpicks to play. The group of sticks are held upright in the hand on the floor or ground, then let go. They will fall in a haphazard manner one upon another and the aim is to pick up the sticks one at a time without the rest moving. Aids were added such as small hooks and much cheating tended to occur.

Sheer strength of the children is tested in games of *Tug-of-War*, whereas it is the size and durability of a chestnut that determines the winner in a game of *Conkers*. This is a European game played in the autumn when the fruit of the horse chestnut tree ripens and falls to the ground. The hard shiny chestnut contained in a prickly outer skin is not edible but makes a good weapon. A conker is made by passing a string through a hole drilled into the chestnut and knotting it at one end. The aim of the game, requiring two or more people each equipped with their favourite conkers, is to smash an opponent's conker by a downward strike. When a player has run out of whole conkers, he retires until he can collect another batch. The winner is the one whose conkers survive.

Many of the 'quieter' games have become party games. There are many hand and hand clapping games, such as *Pat-a-Cake* and *This Little Pig Went to Market*. These could be played with very young children. Many of the games for the very young have quite delightful verses which may create a diversion for a fractious child.

Pat a cake, pat a cake, baker's man!
Bake me a cake as fast as you can;
Roll it and prick it and mark it with a T,
Toss it into the oven for Thomas and me.
[The letter and name are substituted for the child's.]

This little pig went to market
This little pig stayed at home
This little pig had roast beef
This little pig had none.
And this little pig ran all the way home.

This last rhyme has several endings, such as the little pig went 'squeak, squeak, squeak'. Often while reciting the verse the adult will tweak the child's toes or fingers.

Sometimes a bouncing ball was introduced and hand movements had to be achieved while the ball was in the air, an ever-increasing number of movements being added. Hand games could also settle arguments.

A favourite hand game played throughout the world is *Stone, Scissors, Paper*, in which the fist is the stone, the palm the paper and two separated fingers the scissors. Usually played by only two children at a time, each places his hand behind his back. On the count of three, he thrusts his hand out showing one of the hand shapes. The stone wins over the scissors because it could break them, while the scissors over the paper because they could cut and the paper over the stone because it could wrap it up. Generally, the winning numbers are added up and the eventual winner has the greatest number of wins.

Pass the Parcel[1] is another party game that can be played with or without supervision. A 'parcel' in the form of a box or perhaps balloon must be passed from player to player without being handled. Anyone who touches the parcel with his hands or drops it is out of the game. Groups in an outdoor setting also play the game where they find a suitable parcel such as a stick or ball. A rewarding game variation has a parcel wrapped in many layers. As the game progresses the parcel is unwrapped as it passes between the children. The winner receives what is actually in the parcel, possibly a small toy or sweets.

Hunt the Thimble, requiring one object or person to be hidden, can be both an outdoor or indoor game. The player chosen as IT must not see where the object is hidden by the others and must guess where it is following directions, usually in the form of being told they are hot or cold. It is a good lesson on taking and giving orders and keeping one's temper under control.

Simon Says[2] is possibly the best known of the command games. One chosen player determines moves and the rest must follow suit. It may combine hopping, skipping and jumping or may be restricted to body twists while standing on the spot. Not every child is lithe and able to do these movements and the IT player is skilled if he can outdo the others and remain the leader.

Perhaps the best known of the games, requiring neither movement nor equipment, is *I Spy*. Played both indoors and outdoors, even in the car, one player selects an object, announces the first letter of its name with the words: 'I Spy with my little eye something beginning with …' and the rest of the players must guess what he has seen.

Adding Equipment

Over the past 200 years, more organised sports have been introduced, such as ball games. Played under supervision they may be part of a school curriculum but their methods of play can be traced back to the fun children had in deciding their own rules for the games. Tossing a ball from one child to another is a simple game; however, add a bat and suddenly many diverse games could be played from *Cricket* and *Baseball* to *Golf*.

Many of these simple games could be played both indoor and outdoor. By adding a few more pieces of equipment, games that are more complicated may be played. Games using marbles are very numerous, with the winning of marbles from one's opponent the usual aim.

Today most marbles are made of glass, often blown glass in various colours with intricate inner designs. The name itself derives from the material. Small pieces of marble were placed between two large grinding stones. These stones had a spiral channel cut into them which tapered to the centre. As the marble was ground, it was reduced in size and turned into a sphere.[3] Other materials were also used, for example in France, clay 'marbles' painted in bright colours were the norm.

There is indication that Roman children played with marbles and even today many of the games resemble miniature lawn bowling or curling. Players 'shoot' their marbles at targets. Occasionally a larger marble will be used as a jack or target. Other times a target circle or line is marked out and the aim is to be the best or nearest, or even furthest, from the given target. Children carried their marbles in small bags or pouches and today mothers who fear their child might eat them do not appreciate the esteem a marble collection brings to its owner, too prized to be merely eaten.

Played in Europe, Asia and even on Pacific Islands is *Knucklebones*, *Fivestones* or *Jacks*. It is still a favourite game today though its origins go back into antiquity. Originally made from the knucklebones of sheep, the pieces were also cast in different metals. Although the knucklebones could be an aid to fortune telling or gambling, it is as a child's game where they are best remembered.

Several games may be played. However, the most frequent game requires five knucklebones which are tossed into the air.

The aim of the player is to catches as many as possible on the back of his hand. To increase the difficulty, a jack is introduced, usually a small ball. The knucklebones are thrown on the ground and the jack thrown into the air. The aim of the game is to pick up at least one knucklebone and catch the jack before it hits the ground. The game may proceed on the next round to picking up two knucklebones at a time, until the fifth round when the players must pick up all of them. Dexterity and coordination skills are needed to keep an eye on the ball as well as on an irregular pattern on the ground.

Stilt Walking is a game many older children play using homemade platforms from tin cans or sophisticated wooden stilts. Balance and coordination are the ingredients and competitions of skill as well as pretend battles can be played. *Pogo Sticks*, looking for all the world like a bicycle handlebar mounted on a large spring, were introduced in the 1950s and require balance and determination to stay on while hopping about.

Perhaps the game that embodies all the fresh air, running about and skill that children learn through play is *Flying a Kite*. Many children design and make their own kites. The whole family, young and old, can take part in a game. On the other hand, perhaps the most violent of all the games are those where something is thrown. These games have a target to be hit.

The old English game *Aunt Sally* had a carved wooden head drilled with several holes into which were placed objects to be knocked off or broken. Usually, up to the 1950s, clay pipes were the targets. Large sticks were tossed at the head to break the targets. Fun fairs and seaside amusements used the game and it may have the same origins as the less violent indoor games of *Ring Toss* and *Hoop-La*.

Piñata is a symbol of the devil holding all sorts of tempting items. The game derived from an idea that is played at Christmas in Mexico. The figure or piñata is an animal, bird or flower-shaped vessel containing sweets, nuts and small toys. It is hung up in such a manner that it can be moved up and down as well as swaying. The aim is to hit the vessel until it breaks and releases all its goodies.

Games with little or no equipment are those that children play for themselves. The games provide physical development and social development. Games for educational development are much more formal and usually provided by adults.

Games for One or More Players

Games for One Player

There is only one game that is actually designed to be played by oneself and that is *Solitaire*. Many games may be played by only one person but in these cases, that person must assume the roles of all the players that would otherwise be involved.

Solitaire, said to have been an invention of a man held in the Bastille during the French Revolution, is based on a board for the game *Fox and Geese*. It is a cross shape with either thirty-three or thirty-seven holes and thirty-two or thirty-six counters. These counters may be pegs, stones or marbles depending on the holes of the board. All the counters are placed on the board with the exception of the central hole. The aim of the game is to remove all the pegs by jumping over another peg until a single one is left in the central hole. An intriguing game with many versions, it can be an aid to concentration.

The *Tangram Puzzle* is another game for one person, although two may also play it. Consisting of seven square and triangular blocks, the puzzle is to place these in such a position as to create a larger square. During the nineteenth century, booklets were published showing designs that could be created by rearranging the blocks. These blocks then took on almost an architectural use.

Often regarded as time wasters and largely replaced by computer games now, to those who enjoy playing with them, these games are fun and test the patience and ability of the player.

Games for Two Players

Once a second player is introduced, the number of games that can be played is multiplied as the players try to compete against each other. Many of the games are referred to as Strategy Games, as they require more thought and less chance to play. There are several different types of Strategy Games, Hunting Games such as *Fox and Geese*, Alignment Games such as *Nine Men's Morris* and War Games such as *Chess*.

Chess is the best known of the war games. It is played all over the world by all ages and 'both sexes'. There are major national and international competitions as well as ones at local and school levels. One may see the game being played in parks or in coffee houses just for the sheer enjoyment of the participants.

Dominoes is another much loved game for both young and old, although it is generally regarded as an adult's game. China is credited with the origins of *Dominoes* and the game was played there for many centuries before appearing in Europe and gradually spreading from Italy to England. Over the last 200 years many variations were produced, particularly in the last half of the nineteenth century when puzzle and picture games were introduced for families to play with and as teaching aids for children. Even today, makers are producing this game specifically for children.

Garden Games Limited[1] designed *Giant Dominoes* in 2004 and the game is still in production. Made of wood, the game is part of a range of outdoor games of which some are versions of classic games and others designed to work on an outdoor scale.

Hunting Games may or may not have mismatched players. In the case of *Fox and Geese*, there is one fox and thirteen to seventeen geese. The aim of the fox is to capture all the geese, however, it is possible for the geese to encircle the fox and thus win. Played on a cross-shaped board like that of *Solitaire*, the moves may be in any direction from hole to hole. The fox can jump but the geese may not and if one of the geese counters is jumped, it is removed from play. The fox wins when all the geese have been caught or when there are no longer enough geese to trap the fox. It is probable that this game has Viking ancestry rather than coming from the Middle East although the board shape is very alike games such as *Alquerque*.

By adding one fox and almost doubling the number of geese to twenty-four, another game usually called *Asalto* is made. Often based on siege warfare, the greater number attempt to capture a fortified area defended by the two counters. Again the cross-shaped board is used with one of the arm of nine stations representing the fortified area and the twenty-four 'attackers' are placed on the remaining stations. The 'defenders' may move in any direction and jump, thus capturing men – but the men may only move forward. If, however, a possible jump is missed, that counter, the defender, is removed. The 'attackers' win if they trap both 'defenders' or occupy the whole fortified area. Otherwise, the 'defenders' win if they remove so many 'attackers' that the latter is unable to accomplish their win.

During the nineteenth century the game of *Fox and Geese* was adapted to commemorate various wars and battles. This follows many of the race games, which celebrated the exploits of king and country. Of course, service men had always played games while waiting for battles to happen; there was much boring spare time often in horrible conditions between periods of violence. In *The Game of Besieging*, published in Germany at the beginning of the nineteenth century, two armies of twelve men each are represented. The game is played to the same rules and on the same board as *Fox and Geese*. Later in the 1840s, the American company, W. & S.B. Ives of Salem, published two 'fox and geese' games based on the battles between the Crusaders and the Saracens under the titles *The Game of Pope and Pagan or Siege of the Stronghold of Satan by the Christian Army* and *Mahomet and Saladin or The Battle for Palestine*. These two games, long removed in historical times from the events, give an insight into both the political and religious thoughts at the time of publication.

In 1911, the Chad Valley Company of Birmingham, one of the biggest board games publishers during the twentieth century, published a game called *Scouting*, which was dedicated to General Baden Powell's Boy Scouts. Following the rules of *Fox and Geese*, one player is called the dispatch runner. It is his aim to take a note from the field officer to the camp without being captured by a patrol of scouts that have been sent to intercept him. Although a game, it does reflect the use of older boy scouts bridging the gap with the military employed to run messages back and forth, particularly when fighting men were at a premium. Boys were used as runners during the London Blitz by the Fire Brigade when other forms of telecommunications were lost.

The best-known Alignment Game is *Noughts and Crosses*. A simple game, perhaps, but one that can be played anywhere on any surface. Boards may be scratched out on the ground, written on a scrap of paper or be elaborate commercially made wooden, ceramic or plastic ones. By making nine squares from four crossed lines, the game favours the first player; however, he must be skilled enough to form a line of three while stopping his opponent.

The Alignment Game of *Nine Men's Morris* has been much adapted over the centuries. A board has been found on stone slabs in Egypt and another at Troy as well as ones in Ireland. Played throughout Europe where it is usually referred to as *Mérelles*, or mill, *Nine Men's Morris* comes from the number of men each player has to play with; other games using fewer men may also be played. The board has three concentric squares joined by lines forming twenty-four points or stations and it is on the stations that the game is played. The players take turns placing their men, and when all eighteen pieces are on the board, they then take turns to try and form a line of three men, similar to the game of *Go* and the modern game of *Connect*. If a player makes a line, usually a mill hence the name, he is entitled to take one of his opponent's men although he may not take one from a line formed by his opponent unless there are no other men on the board. One of the simpler rules is that if a line is broken by moving one of the men away and then moving it back on the next turn, it forms a new line and the player may take another man. The winner is the player who removes seven of the nine men of his opponent or blocks all the moves available to his opponent. At one time, dice were thrown to decide the play and position of the men but that has not been the practice for several centuries.

A simple game to make with difficult rules is played in many parts of Africa and bears the general name *Yoté*. Again, it is one of capturing opponent's men using a board of twenty-five holes. Children play this game by digging the holes in the ground and having a set number of pebbles or small sticks as counters. One counter is played at a time and it is not necessary to use all the counters. No diagonal moves are allowed but the counters are captured in the same way – by jumping over them. The main difference between this game and the ones already discussed is that a captured counter provides a bonus as another counter may be taken. With astute play, this could mean that one player will quickly win; however, sometimes the game will end in a draw when each player has less than three counters in play.

During the twentieth century, a number of Games of Alignment were published and toward the end of the century, the version is called *Connect*. Intriguing names such as *Peg'ity*, *Spoil Five* and *Quintro* or *5 in a Row* were registered by various makers. These games made of wood and cardboard show both adults and children on the lid design. The aim for each of these games is to form a line of five from counters of the same colour while preventing opponents doing the same.

A rather simple game to play but requiring skill and luck is the *Balance Game*. This is a game to create a tower and there is a semi-circular base on which must be placed a series of five square and round blocks. The placement is determined by the throwing of a specially marked die and as the tower grows its stability decreases. The aim is to hope the tower does not collapse during your turn. There is, however, a rather simple solution to the game, but one not usually thought of before the building has begun.

Games for More than Two Players

Fox and Geese and *Nine Men's Morris* gave rise to a number of games designed for more than two players. One adaptation of *Fox and Geese* may have been the forerunner of *Chinese Checkers*, a game for up to six players. The cross shape is used with each player having a set number of counters. These are placed in two arms of the cross and the aim is to move the counters into the opponent's area by moving around the rest of the board with both single and jump moves. In this game, the counters remain on the board and the winner is the one who first reaches the goal.

Chinese Checkers may be played with up to six people, each with a set of coloured counters. The board is a six-pointed star shape covered with 121 holes or stations and the starting areas in each of the points. The aim is to move all one's counters across the board from one point to the opposite point. For two or three players, fifteen counters each are used; for more than three players, ten counters each are used. Moves are from hole to hole either as single moves or as jumps. A skilled player will build up a string so as many jumps as possible can be made across the board while not giving a helping hand to one's opponents. Played all over the world by children and adults, the game appears to have been derived from *Halma*; however, its true origins are not known. The title has allowed some very fanciful games of *Chinese Checkers* to be published showing dragons and fireworks.

Halma is the Greek word for 'Jump'. In England, F.H. Ayers registered the game and name in 1888, however, do not appear to have made any as J. Jaques & Son and Woolley & Co. and later Chad Valley did. The name and style of the game had been imported from the United States, where George H. Monks and Thomas Hill invented the game in the early 1880s based upon an English game called *Hoppity*. This is a good illustration of how games move from country to country and are adapted for play.

Halma is played on a board with 256 small squares, sixteen along each side. In the corners there are heavy lines marking off each fortified area of thirteen squares, which is also the starting area with two diagonally opposite ones having an extra line marking out nineteen squares. In addition, there are four sets of different coloured counters, two set of nineteen and two sets of thirteen. Originally when issued the counters looked like small wooden chess pawns, but draughtsmen in wood and now in plastic may be used.

The game may be played by two players, three or four players playing separately, or by four players playing as partners. Partnership *Halma* may be played in two ways, the first as pairs with pieces in adjacent areas or as pairs with pieces in the diagonally opposite areas. The latter provides more scope for the partners to help each other. The aim of the game is for each player to attempt to move his counters from his own fortified area into that diagonally opposite. The game is won by the first player or pair to achieve this objective.

Starting positions vary with the forms of play. When there are two players, each takes a set of nineteen pieces and positions the counters in the areas with nineteen squares. When there are three or four players, each one takes thirteen counters and positions them on the thirteen areas. Moving right to left around the board, the players may only move one counter at a time. Moving pieces may be done in any direction – straight or diagonally, forward or backward, to one side or the other into an empty square. Both a single step from square to square may be made or a jump over another counter, either his own or his opponents'. In this game, all the counters as in *Chinese Checkers* remain in play.

An interesting game for a single player of *Halma* is to place nineteen counters in a pattern across the board within nineteen moves. It is said that there are several hundred ways to find the solutions; however, a fairly skilled player should be able to find fifty different solutions.

In the 1920s, an adaptation was published by Hayford & Co., under the name *The New Game of Colorito*. Using a board with 100 squares, sixty of which are in four different colours, the remaining forty opposing squares are numbered one to twenty. With two sets of twenty coloured and numbered discs, the aim of the game is to move the discs from one end of the board to the other and into appropriately numbered squares. The added complication is that while the discs remain in play they must be on their appropriate colour.

With the introduction of moulded plastic towards the end of the twentieth century, three-dimensional games have been produced. *Chess*, *Draughts* and *Noughts and Crosses* have all been adapted to this format. Perhaps it was the use of a three-dimensional game in the television series *Star Trek* that gave rise to many of the games being given 'space' name such as *Spacelines, The 3-D Puzzle of the Future*, which is *Noughts and Crosses*. Of course, many of the games have been adapted for computer use with new graphics and music. Many of these games have the same titles, however, new titles have been introduced but often the methods of play and the rules are the same.

3

Board Games

Not all outdoor games are running and jumping about ones, some may be played on a board. This is not necessarily a wooden or cardboard square but it may be one scratched out on the ground or one etched into stone, it may even be one made of cloth.

The name 'board' really means 'playing surface', that there is a specified area on which the game is played. It defines the method and rules of play and the number of people able to play at any one time. The moves of the majority of the games are governed by the throw of dice. This introduces the element of luck and for the players the possibility of sharing the blame for losing.

Because there is little written or pictorial evidence surviving from antiquity it is very difficult to give the origins of many games, save that the majority are ancient and known to both the Middle and Far East regions. Some games came from China, some on the Silk Route and others via India, Afghanistan and Persia. These were well-travelled areas in antiquity and the games were taken from place to place, sometimes adapted and changed, other times remaining essentially as first played. Other games from India were brought by traders and colonists.

One of the earliest games available to us is shown in the British Museum. It was last played with about 4,500 years ago in the city of Ur. Other games have survived from Ancient Egypt, the *Game of Senet* and the game *Mehen*. Some of the games may have had religious significance; however, mankind's desire to play games probably overruled any objections to the fun or gambling aspects of a game. One can see the comparisons between early games and present-day ones, although it is not always possible to know the ancient rules and modern rules have been applied.

There are several different distinct types of board games, those played by one person such as *Solitaire*, those played by two people or two groups of players such as *Chess* and those played by more than two, such as *Snakes and Ladders*. Of course, any game may be played by one person, who then must take the role of all the players. This is one of the ways experts and enthusiasts study and evolve their own games.

Games from Antiquity

Given the name *The Royal Game of Ur* because it was found in the Royal Tombs of Ur in Mesopotamia by Sir Leonard Woolley in the 1920s, the rules of this game are not known although a number of different suggestions have been put forward by leading games experts. The decorative rosettes found on some boards probably had a purpose during play; however, a number of different games could have been played on the board. The design of the game is complemented by two sets of seven counters or markers made of shell and shale and six dice made in a pyramid shape. The board is hollowed out so it may take all the playing pieces and dice.

Said to be one of the most popular games through-out the ancient world, examples have been found from the Mediterranean and Egypt to India. A version of the game survived within a Jewish community at Cochin in southern India where it was generally played by women. The British Museum has created an online version of the game, which can be played today.

The aim of one of the methods of play is to move all the counters from a start position to the end, thus it becomes a race game. The start is one of the outer rosettes at the bottom of the larger panel, the players taking either the right or left side. The counters move up the board, around the top six squares and straight down the centre squares. It may be that the rosettes are safety squares as counters may be removed to be started again should the opponent's counter land on the same square. Moves are determined by the throw of the dice, three allotted to each player. When this game is played with these rules, one can see the similarity to many children's games, such as *Ludo*; however, it may be because the interpretation of the game has been made by modern scholars.

The *Royal Game of Ur* was the foundation for game boards found in Egypt, in particular the *Game of Twenty Squares*. The board is a different shape – that of a T – with a 4 x 3 panel at the top and a tail of eight squares. Rosettes feature on the board and it is probable that the playing rules are the same. This game is sometimes found with the *Game of Senet* on its reverse side.

Senet is thought to have been one of the most popular games of ancient Egypt. Pharaohs are shown playing it, and very elaborate boards have survived, as well as carvings of the board design in stone done by workmen. These indicate that the game was played across the social scale and the peasants would have scratched the design in the ground. A form of the game is still played today. Like the *Royal Game of Ur*, the British Museum has an online version that can be played.

The aim of the game is to move all one's markers around the board and off it while preventing one's opponent from doing the same, rather like *Ludo*. Played in an S-shape movement, the two players move their five or seven markers around the board. The game has thirty squares in three parallel lines of ten with the last five being marked and designated as safe with the exception of square twenty-seven, when a counter landing on it must start again. A lot of luck and some skill are needed to play the game.

The start position has the ten playing counters, usually black and white, alternately sitting on the first ten squares. The first player, playing black, moves from square ten following the throws of the dice until he throws a two or three when the second player begins. The four dice used are sticks with a white side and a black side.

It is said that the board represents the furrows made by oxen and that the game is a duel between the spirits of the dead in the underworld. Again, the game is similar to recent race games for perhaps the same reason as the *Royal Game of Ur*.

Mehen on the other hand is a spiral race game as it represents a coiled snake. The character was the defender of the Sun Boat, usually portrayed as a man with a serpent head. The game is depicted in Egyptian reliefs together with counters in the shape of lions and lionesses. However, how the game was actually played is not known. Nevertheless, the shape and design of this game produced many variations in eighteenth-century England.

Nard is the ancient game that closely resembles the modern game of *Backgammon*. It is still widely played in many parts of the world and forms of it were certainly played in ancient Greece, the Roman Empire and China. Thought to have been brought to England by the Crusaders and often played as a gambling game in inns and public houses, it was compared as a rival to *Chess*. It is now far from popular but remains a good strategy game for children and a good gambling game for adults.

Another ancient game with its roots in Egypt is *Alquerque*, an early form of *Draughts* or *Checkers* rather than *Chess*; although the board looks like one for guessing how many triangles you can see. It has a pattern of sixteen squares crossed by a diamond and an X; the resulting design gives a pattern of triangles forming twenty-five stations of play. First introduced into Spain by the Moors and described in the famous *Libro de los Juegos* (*Book of Games*) produced for Alfonso X, King of Castile in 1283, it is still played there today with two sets of twelve counters, one white and one black. The counters are arranged on the stations or points of the triangles and play begins. Counters are moved from a station to an empty station. Should this result in jumping over an opponent's counter, that counter is removed from the game. As in *Draughts*, a series of jumps may be made. However, if a piece *could* jump its opponent's and does not, it must be removed. A player loses the game when all his counters have been removed.

Forms of this game can be seen across the world today. In New Mexico, Zuni tribe play *Awithlaknannai*, a double zigzag pattern of sixteen triangles using two sets of twelve counters. It is said to represent snakes and stones and may have been introduced by the Spanish conquistadors. The moves are very similar and the game ends when one player has lost his counters. In Sri Lanka, there is *Peralikatuma*, where four triangles have been added to the sides of the original *Alquerque* board, each with a further six stations. In this game, the players each have twenty-three counters.

With these particular games, one sees the relationship between their designs and those of the games *Solitaire*, *Fox and Geese* and *Nine Men's Morris*.

Yet another board with a history dating back to Egypt is *Mancala*, *Wari* or *Oware*. Although played all over the world, it was in Africa that it was popular and still is. The game was transported to the West Indies by slaves and it is still extremely popular there and within the West Indian communities in England and other countries. It is truly a game that may be played at any time and anywhere. Boards may be made of wood or clay, but may also be simply scooped out of the ground and players can use any type of small bead, shell or dried bean or pea as counters.

The board usually has six compartments for each player and a seventh to hold any counters he might capture, although the aim of the game is to capture the opponent's compartments. Played by experts at great speed, the counters from one compartment are said to be sown one by one into the next compartments in an anti-clockwise direction. A compartment may only be captured when there are two or three counters in it, not at any other time. It may have three or four rows but the rules of play are essentially the same.

Played by men, women, boys and girls, the games are given the general title *Mancala* but they have many different names depending on where you are. There is *Hus* in South Africa, *Bao* in Kenya, *Wari* in the Caribbean and *Olinda Kaliya* in Sri Lanka. Sometimes these titles refer to a range of *Mancala* games played in a certain area, other times to individual games. Like other Strategy Games, there are international and national competitions, though it is still a game to be played for enjoyment.

Other than *Chess*, one of the best-known ancient games still played today is *Go*. Throughout the Far East this game, which has changed little over thousands of years, is still a firm favourite. It may be played on a prepared board or on a surface scratched into the ground. The playing surface is 19 x 19 squares forming 361 points and the play is on these points not within the squares. Thought to be of Chinese origins, it was in Japan where this war-like game was practiced by all with special schools and lessons for the gifted to become masters.

Go is a classic war game between two players using black and white counters. The aim is to capture counters by surrounding them. Once placed on the board, the counters are not moved and others of both colours added. Protective chains of one colour can be made but these may be taken by surrounding the whole chain. If a counter is captured, it is removed from the board. All removed counters are added at the end of the game and the person with the greatest number is the winner. It is not always necessary to surround a counter for it to be captured, if there is one move left to it. However, in these cases, if still in the same position at the end of the game, the counter becomes a captured piece for the totalling of the score.

A simplified version of the game designed for quickness and ease is *Go-Bang*, played on a surface of 13 x 13 squares. In this game, a line of five counters wins. It is the same game as *Tic-Tac-Toe* or modern-day *Connect*.

At the present time, there are still inventors of games. Both physical games and video games are being thought up, developed and being made available to players. With the advances of technology, video games and virtual gaming experiences abound. Nevertheless it has been with amazing ease that old, even ancient, games have been made available on computers and even smartphones. However, these digital versions are often played alone, or with other players joining from anywhere in the world online. No matter how exciting the graphics are, these games – when played alone – seem to lose their edge when players no longer pit their wits against each other but against a mechanical being with an almost limitless memory.

4

Race Games

One of the most enjoyable times to be had by children when they are not racing around is to play Race Games. These games with an element of chance have playing surfaces designed for two or more people. The aim is to win!

This format of game, a race, became the basis for a major industry in England during the eighteenth century and later throughout Europe and the United States. One wonders why perhaps; the answer is quite simple – the games were fun to play. The games' appearance coincided with developments in the printing industry, particularly in England. Mass production was achieved by publishers and it was possible to produce these games at reasonable prices. Astute publishers began to produce games that were educationally sound, they taught history, morals, mathematics, even languages. These attracted the rising middle-class parents who were able to afford the games and felt strongly that their children should be as well educated as possible. Thus, there was a product and a market for it. As the population started to go to school, these subjects were gradually replaced by mere fun ones without losing any of the elements that had made the games so successful.

Many of the early games had an element of gambling too, a central kitty or pool into which penalties were paid and rewards taken. On the other hand, many of the games were played with a small spinning top, a teetotum, instead of dice which were considered an evil influence. Nevertheless, the spinning of the teetotum had the same effect as the dice, it governed the movement of the markers upon the board. Penalties or forfeits and rewards could be given in other ways, sometimes one player paid another, the markers could be moved forward or backward or one had to begin at the start again. Rarely were the markers actually removed from play.

History of the Modern Race Games

The modern race game is attributed to a game with the intriguing name of *Goose*. Based on games seen in the Middle and Far East, it was in Spain that the first appearance of the game was recorded as a gift to King Philip II from Francesco de Medici of Florence, Italy between 1574 and 1587. Within ten years, the game's popularity spread quickly across Europe and it was registered in England by John Wolfe in 1597 as *The Newe and Pleasant Game of the Goose*. Quite why a goose is unknown, it may have some connection to the Golden Goose, but the image of a goose remained a favourite subject for many of the games derived.

The first games of *Goose* had sixty-three squares arranged in an anti-clockwise spiral. Even on these earliest games, a moral tone was set; good and bad events happened along the way that were rewarded or penalised depending on the event. For example, landing on a goose square allowed the player either to double his move forward or to throw again. Landing on a bridge required the payment of counter to the central kitty, while landing in the Ale House one missed a turn. Death was one of the events usually resulting in the player having to start again; this also was the penalty for overshoot-ing the last square.

The Italian game *Il Gioco Dell'Oca* published about 1750 is played in the same manner as other race games and it is very like *Nouveau Jeu de l'Oie*, a French version published about a century later. At the starting point is a woman with keys at a gate and above her head are two children looking out of a window. Square sixty-three, the end, shows a couple dancing before a table laden with food. As well as the good illustra-tions there are other animals and people, together buildings, including the prison at square fifty-two. Rewards and forfeits are required along the path, and the rules are shown in the centre of the game.

Throughout the eighteenth century and again during the nineteenth century, *The Game of Goose* was adapted many times by many different publishers. Generally the spiral remained with more or less the same number of squares. However, occasionally a different theme or image would be introduced. In 1808, John Wallis of London published *The New & Favorite Game of MOTHER GOOSE and the Golden Egg*. Played by the same rules the game is based on the pantomime popular at the time and shows Vauxhall Gardens and St Dunstan's Church in London, together with Grimaldi the Clown who was at the height of his career at the time. The hand-coloured engraving shows Mother Goose flying on a goose in the centre of a spiral of thirty-three squares, sixteen of which have an illustration, eight of which have a golden egg and eight are empty. When a player lands on a golden egg he is rewarded with a counter, however, on a blank square, he must pay a counter to the cen-tral kitty. Some forty years later Richard H. Laurie published *The Royal Pastime of Cupid or Entertaining Game of the Snake*. It may have been inspired by the ancient Egyptian game *Mehen* but is played to the same rules as the goose games.

The publishers of the eighteenth-century English games were concentrated in London, near Fleet Street and

St Paul's Churchyard. They were already supplying books, including children's books, and maps. A number were in fact cartographers and it seems that maps were the basis of the first educational games. There were several great names in the publishing world, some of whom went on for many years, others whose work was reissued many times with small adaptations.

The best-known and probably the most prolific of the publishers was the Wallis Family. John Wallis and his sons, John Jr and Edward, published games and dissected puzzles between 1775 and 1847. Their first address in Ludgate Street was often named the Map Warehouse; later they moved to the Instructive Toy Warehouse in Warwick Square. The last known address was in Skinner Street, Snow Hill, but John Jr also had premises in the Strand and in Sidmouth, Devon at the Marine Library.

Robert Sayer was one of the first of the publishers in London working in Fleet Street. He had a thriving business of material for children, including games and puzzles though many were geographical in design. Starting in 1745, he sold his business to Robert Laurie and James Whittle in 1794 who continued at the same address. Robert Laurie was an engraver by trade, working from the end of the 1770s and the partnership published maps and prints. Much of the work produced by Sayer was reissued repeatedly including *The Royal Pastime of Cupid*. Laurie and Whittle were succeeded by Richard Holmes Laurie after the death of his father in 1812 and the death of James Whittle in 1818. He continued the business in Fleet Street until 1859.

Not all of the publishers were men, Elizabeth Newbery was part of a family producing children's literature. Her own establishment, from 1780, was in St Paul's Churchyard, managed by John Harris who bought it in 1801. The business had the title Original Juvenile Library, reflecting the selling of literature, and it was sold in 1843 to Grant & Griffiths. Many of Elizabeth Newbery's games were issued in conjunction with John Wallis. This is not a rare occurrence; many of the publishers worked with other publishers, engravers, printers and designers to create a game.

The last of the great eighteenth-century publishers was William Darton who established his company in Gracechurch Street in 1785. The company had various names depending on who was the senior partner, W. Darton & Co., Darton & Harvey when Joseph Harvey joined in 1791, Darton, Harvey & Darton when William Darton's son Samuel joined in 1811 and back to Harvey & Darton when William died in 1819. It switched between Darton & Harvey and Harvey & Darton before the company was sold in 1847. All the different names give a guide to the dates of production, especially when a publishing date is missing or the game was reissued later. All these names must not be confused with those of William Darton Jr who opened his own business in Holborn Hill in 1804 and worked until 1866. He also had a number of different imprints including W. & T. Darton, William Darton & Son, and Darton & Clark. Between them, the Darton companies were prolific publishers of children's games and puzzles, many educational but some just fun to play.

William Spooner, born in the eighteenth century, was a leading publisher of the nineteenth century, working from 1831 to 1854 at addresses in the Strand and Regent Street. Using primarily trade and manufacturing subjects, rather than geography and history, he was one of the first to use lithographs rather than engravings. Many of his designs were quite humorous. For example, in his game issued in 1848 under the title *The Cottage of Content or Right Roads and Wrong Ways*, a decidedly moral game, there is reference to Laughing Stock Lane where boys are laughing at a man in the stocks.

During the nineteenth century, more and more games were imported from Germany. While the English companies were quick to embrace the new technology of the steam-driven printing presses of the eighteenth century, they were slow to adapt to the changes of the next century. On the other hand, German publishers, or English publishers with factories in Germany, quickly took on the new developments and by the 1860s were taking the market by storm printing coloured lithographs instead of the hand-coloured engravings. The price came down but so did the quality both of the games themselves and the subject matter. Except for the morals connected with *Snakes and Ladders*, all the educational themes were removed.

J.W. Spear & Sons was one London-based company, founded in 1878, which had factories in Nuremberg, Germany and continued in business up to the late 1990s. Although producing board games, the company was better known for many of its table games and educational craft kits. On the other hand, John Jaques & Son, established in Hatton Gardens in 1849 published a wide range of board games together with card and table games; the company is now better known for its sports equipment.

The Chad Valley Company of Birmingham was established about 1820 as a lithographic, engraving, printing and book-binding business of Anthony Bunn Johnson. In 1897, the sons and grandsons of the founder moved to a new factory in a small village called Harborne, by a stream called Chad and changed the name to Chad Valley. At this point, while maintaining it production of stationers' sundries, the company introduced a range of board games. Increasingly throughout the twentieth century toy production including dolls gathered strength but by 1979 the company had become a part of General Mills, which also owned a number of American toy manufacturers. In the mid-1980s, Chad Valley ceased production of all its products, including the large enamelled advertising panels used at railway stations.

John Waddington & Company, founded in 1905 was another large English publisher and printer of games and jigsaws. In the 1930s, the company introduced the spelling card game *Lexicon* and in 1995 the craze game *Pog*. It acquired one of its main competitors in 1966, Tower Press, which had printed many card games and jigsaw puzzles.

Many of the games published by The Chad Valley Company and by John Waddington Ltd, together with those by Parker Brothers of the United States are still available as the companies became part of Hasbro. Hasbro of America has a long history in the world of manufacturing dolls, toys and games.

A Note of Caution

Before proceeding further, a note of caution is raised about the use of dice. Many eighteenth-century games will forbid the use of these small six-sided squares. Said to be evil and items of the devil, dice were often found in the household, as it was fine for adults to use them. The game publishers felt that children would be encouraged to gamble.

One of the most common games played by young and old alike using dice was *Hazard*, a forerunner of dice games played in casinos. The game dates back for more than three centuries. Using two dice, the first player, called the Shooter, rolls the dice. If he turns up two, three or twelve, he loses his turn; but with any other number, he continues until he throws the same number as his first roll and wins to carry on the next game, or until he throws a seven in which case he loses. The game continues until all players have had a chance to be the Shooter and the winner is the player with the most rounds.

In America, children developed a game of dice based on the game *Baseball*, appropriately enough called *Baseball Dice*.

Probably created for the winter months, only one die is used and a baseball diamond must be drawn on a sheet of paper or other suitable surface. The diamond is marked 1, 2, 3 and Home Base. The first player is 'at bat' and he throws the die. If the die shows, one to four, the player's marker is moved to that number on the diamond; if, however, five or six is thrown, he is out and the next player takes on the batting and the die. The rest of the throws advance the players around the diamond and as they come to the Home Plate, they score a run. Played over nine games or innings, following the baseball line, an inning lasts until there are three throws of five or six by any of the players. The winner is declared at the end of the game as the one who had the most home runs.

Games for Juveniles of 'Both Sexes'

In the eighteenth century, the educational race games were aimed at an audience no older than twelve. However, it was assumed that the games would be played by all the children of a family and indeed that the whole family would be involved. Many of the games were issued with booklets giving details of each of the squares being played and it was the intention that a child landing on a particular square would read aloud its details.

The teaching process did not stop at merely learning facts; it required reading and speaking abilities too. When read today some of the facts are wrong or misleading. It must always be remembered that the games reflect the attitudes of their time, an outward-looking prosperous Protestant England with London classified as the first city. The world-wide exploration was reaping new species, food and cultures. It is not surprising that many of the games actually made use of the new ideas and were regularly updated.

The education started with geography. Many of the publishers already produced maps and it was a simple adaptation to make a map into a game. When the first geographical games were published, there were areas in the world that had either not been discovered or mapped and some of the maps refer to the Habitable World. Great sways of central Africa and the west coast of North America had yet to be discovered by European travellers. As regions were found and mapped, so were the games updated. Amazingly, most were well informed and enlightened. For example, in a game by John Betts he stated that Sebastian Cabot *rediscovered* Newfoundland in 1496 and strongly disapproved of selling spirits and gunpowder to the North American Indians.

Robert Sayer and John Wallis published maps of England and Wales, Scotland and Europe which they transformed into games. If one compares two published about the same time it is noticeable how similar they are. The formal squares have been replaced with numbered spots. Each map is made of sixteen printed paper panels mounted on a sheet of linen for stability and durability. The design was a hand-coloured engraving with letterpress down each side giving the rules of play and instructions about each of the places 'visited' on the map.

Robert Sayer published his map on 1 June 1787 with the grand title *A New Royal Geographical Pastime for England and Wales* and with the even grander subtitle 'Whereby the Distance of each Town is Laid Down from London in Measured Miles Being a very amusing Game to Play with a Teetotum, Ivory Pillars and Counters'. In this case, the pillars referred to are the men used on the board and the counters are round discs to pay the kitty and any penalties. The map also bears the name of the sculptor CREED. There are 169 towns and the accompanying text describes them and notes any rewards or penalties to be made. The text is quite amazing as cathedrals and churches, stately homes and public buildings are 'visited', and local customs, geography and folklore described. In this game the rewards are forward movement, however, the forfeits or penalties are harsh, usually a payment of a counter to the kitty *and* a backward move.

The game starts with each player placing a set number of counters into the central kitty; this will be taken by the winner. Each player spins the teetotum and moves according to the number spun. Each player must then follow the directions given in the text and read aloud any descriptions. Should a penalty be paid it goes to the kitty. Some of the movement penalties are harsh, moving from near the finish back to the start. If the player overshoots the end number, he must start again but the rules do allow him to move his man backward from his last position by the number spun.

Seven years later, on 24 December 1794, John Wallis published his game with the title *Wallis's Tour Through England and Wales, A New Geographical Pastime*. It bears the name of the sculptor McIntyre as well as the date. Like the Sayer's map, it has sixteen printed paper panels mounted on linen. The descriptive text in letterpress is on each side. The descriptions of the town in this game tend to be commercial, stressing the business or manufacturing aspect of a town rather than its cultural side.

Played in the same manner this game has only 117 spots, the men or playing markers are pyramids of different colours which have four matching counters. These are not placed in a kitty; however, throughout the game one of the penalties is to miss a turn. At that point, a request for a set number of counters is made, and at each of the player's turns to spin, he collects one counter but does not spin, until all are collected. Also in this game, an unlucky traveller who goes to the Isle of Man may be shipwrecked, in which case he leaves the game.

John Wallis published a companion game, *Wallis's Tour of Europe*, which was played in the same manner. Historically it is very interesting as it was published at the height of the Grand Tour and all the best places to visit are included. Yet it shows a Europe quite different to the present-day one and many of the countries named are known by quite different names now.

In the text of these two games, it is revealed that the games were not always sold with the markers and counters. The text states:

Two or three persons may amuse themselves with this agreeable pastime, and if a double set of Counters and Pyramids are purchased, six may play at it. The Totum must be figures 1 to 8 on its several faces, in pen and ink. The pyramids are supposed to be the travellers who make the tour; each pyramid having 4 counters of the same colour belonging to it, which are called markers or servants: when you find that these are complete, you may begin the game agreeable to the following rules.

And so the rules of play are given. It is interesting that when someone would make a tour of either Great Britain or Europe it was assumed that he took a servant with him.

In conjunction with his sons Wallis published another geographical game in 1815, which moved from the map design to the spiral design. Called *The Panorama of Europe, A New Game*, it was a hand-coloured engraving with twelve panels mounted on linen. Numbered in an anti-clockwise direction from one to forty, it started in the lower left corner and finished in the centre with a large panorama of London from Westminster to Wapping as seen from the Surrey side of the River Thames.

There are no known rules with the game, but it is undoubtedly played in the usual manner, with the various hazards and penalties being listed in a booklet describing the various towns or places together with the rules. As with many of the games, the city names differ in spelling to the modern-day names; also country borders have changed in the past 200 years.

Numbered compartments are:

1. Oporto; 2. Lisbon; 3. Madrid; 4. Gibraltar; 5. Malta; 6. Messina; 7. Naples; 8. Rome; 9. Florence; 10. Venice; 11. Paris; 12. The Hague; 13. Rotterdam; 14. Amsterdam; 15. Copenhagen; 16. Hamburg; 17. Dantzic; 18. Preslaw; 19. Ratisbon; 20. Berlin; 21. Magdeburgh;

22. Osnaburgh; 23. Bonn; 24. Leipsig; 25. Dresden;
26. Presburgh; 27. Vienna; 28. Constaninople;
29. Moscow; 30. Petersburgh; 31. Stockholm; 32. Bergen;
33. Glasgow; 34. Edinburgh; 35. Dublin; 36. (Rome)
in corner; 37. (London) in corner; 38. (Paris) in corner;
39. (St. Petersburgh) in corner; 40. London

It was very rare for any of the publishers to express bigotry or make rude remarks about anyone, save the King, however, in 1810 W. & T. Darton published a map of Europe on behalf of its author entitled *Walker's New Geographical Game Exhibiting A Tour Through Europe*.[1] The statements are in marked contrast to ones made about the same time by other authors and publishers.

The game is a hand-coloured engraving mounted on linen and shows the capitals, major cities and the sea routes around Europe. Its accompanying booklet gives detailed descriptions of all the numbered sites:

DIRECTIONS FOR MAKING THE TOUR OF EUROPE.

Two or three persons may amuse themselves with this agreeable pastime; and, if a double set of counters and pyramids are purchased, six may play at it.

The totum must be marked 1 to 8, on its several faces, with pen and ink. The pyramids are supposed to be the travellers who take the tour; each pyramid having 4 counters of the same colour belonging to it, which are called markers or servants; when you find these are complete, you may begin the game agreeably to the following.

RULES:

I. Each player must hold a pyramid or traveller and four counters of the same colour.

II. In order to know who begins the game, each player must spin the totum, and the highest number takes the lead, then the next highest, &c.

III. The first player then spins, and if he turns up No. 4, he is to place his pyramid upon Liverpool, and stay there until it is his turn to spin again.

IV. If, in the next spin, he turns up No. 3, he is to add that to 4, his former number, and place his pyramid on No. 7 (Cork) and in this manner the game must be continued till the traveller arrives at No. 133 (Athens), when he wins his game.

V. If the last spin does not exactly make the No. 133, but goes beyond it, he must then go back as many numbers as he exceeds it and try his fortune again, till one of the players spins the lucky number.

VI. When a player is obliged to wait one or more turns, he must deposit as many counters as he is directed to wait turns (which never exceeds four) when it is his turn to spin again, instead of spinning he must take up a counter and so on till all have been taken up.

In *European Travellers, An Instructive Game*, a rarely documented event is included, the Turkish Janissary rebelling against the Sultan in 1823. There is a change to the method of play. Gone are the teetotum and expensive markers as Edward Wallis indicates in the rules of the game:

The players are provided with a Card, containing nine Letters, nine Numbers, two Crosses and one Blank, which are to be cut up on the lines with a pair of scissors.

The letters are to be distributed one to each player, according to the number about to play, and the remainder laid aside. They are used to mark each player's position on the Game.

The numbers, crosses and blank are to be placed in a lady's reticule, and drawn in turn, one by each player, after the manner of a lottery.

Each player, on drawing a number, is to place his letter on the same number in the Game, and read the description aloud. When it is his turn to draw another, he adds them together and advances his letter to that number which they make when so added, reading as before, and observing any directions which may be given him. But if he draw a cross, he is to draw again, till he obtain a number, which number is to be deducted from, instead of added to his former station, and his letter moved back accordingly. Each card to be returned to the bag after drawing.

Whoever draws a blank, remains at his former number.

After each player has drawn once, the Game is to be continued in the same manner, passing the bag round, till some one makes up the exact number 123 who wins the Game.

If a player go beyond No. 123, he must go as many back as he had exceeded it, and the lottery must continue till some one makes up the exact number.

If two players arrive at the same number, the one who arrived last must go back to his former number.

When a player is sent back to any place, he is not to read the description, or attend to the directions in italics, and when sent forward he is only to read the description and stop there till his turn to draw again.

The Travellers of Europe With Improvements and Additions is based on a game first issued in 1842 by William Spooner. Ten years later, he revised the game which is made of nine lithographs on linen. The text and the rules indicate the thoughts at the time for both the education and enjoyment value of these games and how much diligence the publishers exerted to make the games worthy. A sample of the descriptive text is shown at the end.

PREFACE TO THE BOOKLET OF RULES.
The compiler of 'The Travellers', who has on many occasions successfully catered for the entertainment of youth, has in the present game, aimed at the higher object of

blending instruction with amusement; and while he has attempted to impart the elements of geographical knowledge to very young learners, he has not neglected to make the medium as pleasant and amusing as that of any one of his former popular games. The Study of Geography, in itself so interesting, when pursued through the formal details of a chart, may not at first offer an attraction to the youthful student; but by means of an emulative game, in which the distances and positions of the various countries and capitals are geographically defined, and in which the leading cities of Europe are illustrated by correct representations, the publisher has thought to stimulate the young inquirer to that thirst after knowledge, which may be perfected in maturer years.

The pictorial illustrations of cities are derived from the most recent views on approved authorities, as the Whale Fishery in the Northern Ocean, and the Giant's Causeway in Ireland; or some peculiar custom is portrayed, as sledge travelling in Russia, and the perilous sports of the remote inhabitants of Finland and of Siberia.

Little, it is presumed, need be said in favour of a mode of information at once so pleasing and so exact; or of an amusement which will leave on the youthful mind many of the solid advantages of a more regular instruction. The publisher, therefore, presents this little game with equal confidence both to parents and to children, in the full assurance that to the former it will afford all the satisfaction, and to the latter all the amusement, which either he or they can desire. To those little wayfarers who, by so many various routes, seek the object of the heart's constant affections – Home – he recommends not only the patience and perseverance of more matured travellers, but that as they meet or cross each others' path on this extended stage of travel, they should cultivate that kindness and good humour which sweeten the path of life – to the child as

well as to the man – in the city and in the desert, as well as
by their own cheerful and contented firesides.

The Travellers or a Tour Through Europe/Description of the Game:

The Travellers who are of different nations, having jour-
neyed in company home to the capitals of their respective
countries, by embarking each from some different city in
Africa, or on the shore of the Mediterranean Sea.

The Austrian (distinguished by the mark A) is to start
from Jerusalem; The Russian (marked B) from Cairo; the
Swede (marked C) from Alexandria; the Prussian (marked
D) from Tripoli; and the Englishman (marked E) from
Morocco.

Close to, or upon, these cities, the points of starting are
marked S, and each traveller places his mark or counter on
the part of the city from which has to commence his journey. Their journeys are to be pursued by the turning up
of the totum, which is marked with the letters N, E, S, W
representing north, east, south and west; and each traveller
is to move along the lines of the pictorial map from cross
to cross of the squares as may be determined by the totum.

If the totum turns up:

N: the player moves north or upwards to the next corner,
or crossing of the lines, in a direct road above him; if:

E: he moves to the next corner, or crossing of the lines,
on the right or east; if

S: he moves to the corner immediately below or
south; if

W: he is to move to the next corner to his left or west.

All these movements must be along the lines; and each
time not further than the first crossing of the lines. It must

be well understood that N indicates North or Upward, E – East or right, S – South or downward, W – West or left.

The destination of each traveller is shewn by a circle having the letter of the mark of the player.

Rules:

Draw lots to determine who shall play first, second, third etc.

Each player is to put three counters into the pool on commencing the game.

When a player is directed to move to a crossing or angle occupied by another player; they are to change places with each other.

When a player is so near the margin of the map he can not find an angle or cross to move when directed, he will wait till his next turn to play.

Forfeits are to be paid to, and the prizes taken from the pool, according as the players reach the places where they are named.

Whoever arrives at, or passes over, any part of the capital of a kingdom which is marked and fails to name the country of which it is the capital, is to pay two counters into the pool, and the first player in each game is to hold the book and to enforce the fines at the time, or to pay one counter himself to the pool for every neglect.

When every player has travelled to the extreme part of the North, so as to his mark to within two moves in any direction of his own capital. (This rule is made in order to abridge the duration of the game and to give variety and it may either be adopted or not, as the players may determine when they commence the game).

The traveller who first reaches the capital of his country by passing along the lines that has the circle corresponding with his mark, wins the game and takes the contents of the pool.

Fines and rewards are indicated on the playing sheet at the intersections of various lines of latitude and longitude.

GEOGRAPHICAL DESCRIPTION
The Earth or Globe, consisting of land and water, – the former of which comprehends four grand divisions, called Europe, Asia, Africa and America, – may be represented either in the whole or in part, by geographical charts or maps. The Division our pictorial map attempts to illustrate, is Europe – the smallest but the most civilized of the four quarters of the world.

It is bounded on the north by the Arctic Ocean; on the west by the Atlantic Ocean; on the south by the Mediterranean Sea and the Black Sea; and on the east by Asia.

The following countries comprise the various Divisions of Europe:-

LAPLAND – divided into Swedish and Russian Lapland

SWEDEN and NORWAY – DENMARK

RUSSIA in EUROPE – POLAND-FINLAND

GERMANY – consisting of the Empire of Austria, the Kingdom of Prussia, and the States of Germany

HOLLAND – BELGIUM

GREAT BRITAIN – comprehending England, Wales and Scotland

IRELAND

FRANCE – SWITZERLAND –ITALY

SPAIN – PORTUGAL

TURKEY in EUROPE – GREECE

1. LAPLAND – Part of which belongs to Russia and part to Sweden, is the most northern country in Europe, and is divided into North, South and East Lapland. The climate is very cold, and the country mountainous, with immense forests of fir, and tracts of land covered with moss. The natives are in a very rude state of civilization;

and the whole amount of the population is supposed not
to exceed 60,000.

In the northern part of Lapland the differences in the
length of day and night are greater than in any other part
of the inhabited world. The longest day in summer is about
eight weeks, during which period the sun never sets; and
in winter the longest night continues for a similar period.

William Spooner published a wide range of games and some
of his more intriguing games were *World Travellers of Asia*,
Eccentric Excursion to the Chinese Empire and *Pirates and Traders
of the West Indies*. In the 1840s, Spooner published a game
that he referred to as *THE WONDERS OF THE WORLD,
Chiefly in Reference to the Architectural Works of the Ancients, AN
ENTIRELY NEW GAME for the Amusement and Education
of Youth*. The game is a hand-coloured lithograph, twelve
panels mounted on linen. It shows an overall pictorial image
of ancient, classical and more recent architecture from Egypt,
Petra, to St Peter's in Rome and St Paul's in London. It also
includes a brightly coloured Islamic arch which was possibly
the Alhambra, Spain.

Throughout the nineteenth century and into the
twentieth, geographical games continued to be published.
Sometimes they reflected world travel, other times historical events. England, fascinated by the Far East and its
colonies published *A Tour through the British Colonies and
Foreign Possessions* and *Dioramic Game of the Overland Route to
India*. The first, published by John Betts about 1850, shows
a spiral with London in the centre; he called London the
metropolis of the British Empire and provided both the
overland route and the sea route to India. Travelling around
the world and stopping at thirty-seven places, the game
starts with Heligoland and includes Malta, Sierra Leone,
towns in India, Australia and Canada, and the islands of the

Caribbean. The accompanying booklet describes each place with good and bad comments about the area or the people.

RULES AND DIRECTIONS

I. Appoint one of the party to preside, whose duty it will be to read the description from the book; which office need not preclude his joining in the game.

II. The party will then arrange themselves round the table, in the order in which they intend to play; and each is to be provided with a traveller. Should there be more players than travellers provided, a thimble or small coin will answer the purpose of a traveller.

III. The first player is now to spin, and to place his traveller at the same number on the game as that turned up by the teetotum; when the description given in the book is to be read aloud.

IV. The remaining players are to follow in turn, and spin, and otherwise proceed as directed in Rule III, until it has gone entirely round; when the first is to spin again; and, adding the number now turned up to his former number, he is to shift his traveller on the game accordingly. The other players are to proceed in like manner, continuing until one of them arrives at No. 37 (the British Metropolis), and thus wins the game.

V. Any player going beyond No. 37 must return back as many numbers as he has preceded it.

VI. Two or more players may occupy the same number on the game, with detriment to each other. It seems almost needless to say, that the directions to stop or spin again at certain numbers, are to be observed.

VII. Any player coming to a number with an asterisk (*), must proceed by the numbers with asterisks so long as they last, which will take them to India by way of the overland route – as Malta, Alexandria, Aden, Bombay.

The other will proceed by way of Sierra Leone, Ascension,
St. Helena, and the Cape.

These rules differ from many of the games of this period – the
reading of the descriptions by only one player, no forfeit for
landing on the same number as another and the use of both an
overland route and a sea route to India.

The thirty-seven areas or countries represented were all
British colonies at the time and the list comprises these:

1. Heligoland
2. The Channel Islands
3. Gibraltar
4*. Malta
4. Sierra Leone
5*. Alexandria[2]
5. Ascension
6*. Aden
6. St Helena
7*. Bombay
7. Cape of Good Hope
8. Mauritius
9. Ceylon
10. Madras
11. Calcutta
12. Bengal
13. Malacca
14. Hong Kong
15. Sarawak
16. Western Australia
17. Adelaide
18. Melbourne
19. Van Diemen's Land or Tasmania
20. Sydney
21. Norfolk Island

22. New Zealand
23. Falkland Islands
24. Belize or British Honduras
25. Guiana
26. Trinidad
27. Barbados
28. Jamaica
29. Bermudas or Somers Island
30. Quebec
31. Niagara
32. Canada (North America)
33. Hudson's Bay
34. Newfoundland
35. New Brunswick
36. Nova Scotia
37. London

As with all the games published at this time, the statements given may seem factually wrong, often intolerant and very patronising. However, such statements must be seen within the confines of the historical point of view and not through twenty-first-century ideals. The publishers were Protestant, Anglo Saxons who were very loyal to their country and its government but on the other hand felt they could criticise all if need be. Nevertheless many of the points stated are very tolerant though patronising.[3]

On the other hand, some statements are very poorly thought out such as the ones about the first port of call, Heligoland:

Heligoland is a group of two small islands off the coast of Denmark, to which country they formerly belonged. Perhaps some of our young travellers may think it almost needless to have crossed the German Ocean on purpose to visit these islands, the larger of which is only about

2½ miles in circumference; but as some of them might not have known that Great Britain can boast these possessions, the voyage may not have been entirely in vain. The islands are situated about 30 miles from the mouth of the river Elbe, and on the larger is erected an excellent lighthouse, which is visible nearly 30 miles distant. The inhabitants are principally of the humbler class, subsisting chiefly by fishing and pilotage; and number about 2,000.

At the same time, 1822, William Darton published *The Noble Game of the Elephant and Castle or Travelling in Asia during which the Sagacious Animals introduce us to Various and Instructive Scenes*.[4] At the first spot, a northern area of Russia, the recent finding of a mammoth is discussed with the statement, '... probably they have lain there since the universal deluge when Noah and his family were preserved.' Again there is reference to knowing the time of the flood and also that there was some doubt as to the authenticity of the mammoth. However, the author concluded that the mammoth had been real but did not know the time of its existence. The comments on the people and other cultures is very marked as 'this is abhorrent to the English', but almost acceptable because they were not English.[5]

The booklet contains a letter of explanation, the rules, the descriptions and a poem under the title 'A Caution or Friendly Hint'. The letter was addressed to Lord Henry Russel and proceeds as:

The Publisher offers this Juvenile Game of Amusement and Instruction, in token of the respect he entertains for every branch of the House of RUSSEL.

The useful and improving must ever be acceptable to the Son of the Duke of Bedford; for the example of his late excellent Uncle, with that of his worthy and liberal-minded Father, will naturally lead to the advancement of the Junior branches, who, in following their steps, are sure to pursue the only path to public esteem and private happiness. Thus supported, the dawning abilities of their Son, will, no doubt, ripen to the satisfaction and honour of his amiable Parents; and he who now finds entertainment in a work like the present, may prove a bright and virtuous ornament to a name his ancestors have rendered truly noble.

That the fair promise of his youth may thus be matured, is the hearty wish of his sincere friend, William Darton // Holborn Hill // 4th of 3rd Month (March), 1822.

The game starts with the following under the title 'Directions':

FOUR Persons may amuse themselves at this agreeable Pastime. The Teetotum must be marked One to Eight on its several Faces. The Game may be begun agreeably to the following:

Rules

I. EACH Player must have a Traveller and Four Counters of the same colour.

II. Spin for the first player; the highest Number to begin the Game, when he or she is required to read to the Company 'THE CAUTION' on page 4 of this Book, before the Game is opened.

III. Let the first player spin, and place his or her Traveller on the Game, according to the number turned up. The others, in turn, are to do the same; referring to the explanation for a Description of the Plates.

IV. At each following spin, add the Number turned up to that on which the Traveller stands; and proceed accordingly till some one arrive at No. 25, (A Gentoo) and wins the GAME.

V. Whoever goes beyond No. 25, shall go back as many as he exceeds it; and try again when his turn comes.

VI. When directed to stop one or more turns, the player is to place as many counters on his Number, and take one up each time, instead of spinning, till all be redeemed.

VII. When the spinner reads an Article which has a Note, he or she must refer to the page of Notes for an explanation, and read the same aloud.

These rules refer to both male and female players, many rules do not. While the first player must read the poem 'A Caution', unlike the previous game, the rest of the players must read the descriptions of each of the numbers they land on.

'The Caution' deals with cheating and gambling, both to be considered abhorrent to the players. However, gambling was quite permissible for the adults of a family and often the Travellers and counters used to play these children's games would be gaming pieces.

A CAUTION OR FRIENDLY HINT
Before in this game we proceed
Permit me a few words to say;
I will not five minutes exceed,
Or detain you, good folk, from your play.
I trust all around me are friends,
And will take what I say in good part;
Should word of my Caution offend,
It would grieve me indeed to the heart.
But I wish to pat all on their guard
Against certain tricks I have seen;
And think not my censure too hard,
When I call them both cunning and mean.
I observe even those whom I love,
If they like not the number they spin,
Will the counter or Teetotum move,
In hope by such cheating will win.
But even in trifles like these,
Such conduct should never take place;
Mean actions get on by degrees,
Till they end in our total disgrace.

Besides, though we call this a game,
We cannot but quickly discern
It's only a sport as to name,
In the play, there is something to learn;
Improvement with mirth is design'd
And the least we can do for such care,
While the moral sinks deep in the mind,
Is to play its rules open and fair.
The gambler all hate and despise;
For he plays but to cheat and to gain;
But we to be better and wise;
And neither to cause, nor feel pain.
Well, now I have finished my task,
And should any be tempted to wrong;
I have only one favour to ask,
That they pause and reflect on my song.

By the twentieth century, the games included new methods of transport: trains, bicycles, cars and aeroplanes. One could take a trip from London to Edinburgh on a train, fly across the Atlantic, travel around Africa in the footsteps of Dr Livingstone, tour the London Underground and visit Venice in a gondola.[6]

History Made Easy

One of the most formidable games in the publishers' repertoire taught history. Again these games were an eighteenth-century product lauding the best that was British at the time, the achievements of exploration and colonisation and the wonders of science. Unlike the geography games, ones based on history had a limited life, ending about the middle of the nineteenth century. Perhaps Queen Victoria was not as noteworthy as her predecessors, but she, as a young woman, was the last to be acclaimed in a game. History was an ideal subject for a spiral race game as it could be divided up into specific periods of time and documented events.

The games usually started History with the Norman Conquest of 1066, however *Wallis's New Game of Universal History and Chronology*, published in 1814 daringly started with Creation dated Anno Mundi 1 and included the Great Flood at Anno Mundi 1656. One wonders now how this knowledge, so firmly stated in the text, has been lost over the last 200 years. The accompanying booklet had descriptive texts for each of the 138 squares made of twelve paper panels mounted on linen. In the centre is an image of George, Prince of Wales. He, like his father, was portrayed in many games. The game itself was played by the same rules with forfeits and rewards and when a player was directed to read the history of any event, he was rewarded with a counter from each player and a second spin of the teetotum. In the 1840s, the game was reissued with the centre image being replaced with five including George as King, William IV, Queen Victoria and her marriage with the central one a railway.

CHRONOLOGY OF THE MOST REMARKABLE
EVENTS, From the Creation to the present Time.

Anno Mundi

1.	-1. The creation of the World.
129.	-2. Abel slain by his brother Cain.
1656.	-3. Universal Deluge. *Begin again*.
1757.	-4. Building of Babel. *Pay 3 to the Pool*.
1787.	-5. The Babylonish and Assyrian Monarchies founded. *Read the history, in page 12*.
1816.	-6. Kingdom of Egypt. *Read in page 12*.
1860.	-7. Kingdom of Sicyon founded. *Read in page 12*.
2182.	-8. Letters first invented by Memnon, the Egyptian. *Receive 1 from each player*.
2289.	-9. Fire first struck from flints in Prometheus. The Ancients fabled he stole it from Heaven.
2433.	-10. Birth of Moses, the Jewish Historian. *Read their history, page 13*.
2448.	-11. Kingdom of Athens founded. *Pay 1 to Rome, your more successful rival, at No. 18*.
2519.	-12. The first ship which appeared in Europe brought from Egypt to Danaus.
2811.	-13. Trojan War. *Read in page 14*.
2822.	-14. Eneas flying from Troy, lands in Italy, whence the Romans pretended to derive their origin.
3029.	-15. Ten tribes of Jews revolt. *Pay 2 to the Pool*.

3097.   -16. Homer flourished. *If you can say who he was, and what he wrote receive 1 from each player; otherwise, place 3 on No. 13 and leave there.*

3110.   -17. Money first made of gold and silver at Argos.

3252.   -18. Rome founded. *Read in page 14.*

3403.   -19. A battle between Medes and Lydians, who are separated by a great eclipse of the sun, predicted by Thales.

3442.   -20. Comedies first performed at Athens, by Thespis, on a movable scaffold.

3466.   -21. Babylon taken by Syrus, as predicted by Daniel, in Jewish prophet.

3478.   -22. The public library first founded in Athens. *Spin again.*

3523.   -23. Defence of Thermopylae by Leonidas, with 300 Spartans, against Xerxes with five millions of soldiers.

3589.   -24. The history of the Old Testament ends about this time.

3604.   -25. Socrates, the greatest heathen philosopher, condemned to die by poison, in the 70th year of his age. *Stop one turn to lament the ingratitude of his countrymen.*

3619.   -26. Rome plundered by the Gauls.

3668.   -27. Alexander the Great flourished. *Pay 1 to No. 7 and learn who he was, unless you already know.*

3674.   -28. Death of Darius Codomannus, the last king of Persia. *Pay 2 to your conqueror, at No. 27.*

3719.   -29. Dionsius of Alexandria flourished. He was the first who calculated the exact length of the year, which is 365 days, 5 hours and 49 minutes.

3855.   -30. Carthage in Africa taken and destroyed by the Romans. *Pay 1 to No. 18.*

3916.   -31. Civil war at Rome, between Sylla and Marius: the former is proclaimed perpetual dictator. *Pay 1 to your country at No. 18.*

3950.   -32. Britain first invaded by Julius Caesar.

3960.   -33. Julius Caesar assassinated in the senate house at Rome. *Stop one turn.*

3996.   -34. The city of Rome, at this time, was 50 miles in circumference, and contained upwards of four millions of inhabitants capable of bearing arms.

4000.   -35. Jesus Christ, the Messiah, born, four years before the commencement of the vulgar Christian era. Universal peace prevails. *Take half the Pool, and spin again.*

ANNO DOMMINI

31.   -36. The twelve Apostles chosen to propagate the glad tidings of salvation.

33.   -37. The crucifixion and resurrection of our Lord. *Stop here 2 turns to lament his sufferings, and receive 1 from each player for the blessings derived from them.*

19.   -38. London supposed to have been founded by the Romans.

51.   -39. Caractacus, a British prince, carried prisoner to Rome.

63.   -40. Christianity supposed to have been introduced into Britain by St. Paul, or some of his disciples.

64.   -41. Rome set on fire by command of Nero, who made this a pretence for the first persecution of the Christians. *Stop two turns.*

70.   -42. Jerusalem destroyed by the Romans, according to the prediction of our Saviour. *Place 1 on No. 35*

79.   -43. The cities of Herculanaeum and Pompeii overwhelmed by an eruption of Mount Vesuvius. *Go on to No. 119.*

135.   -44. Termination of the second Jewish war, when they were all banished from Judea. *Pay 2 to No. 18.*

158.   -45. The title of Pope bestowed on the first bishop of Rome. *Go to No. 60.*

222.   -46. The Romans purchase peace with the Goths, by an annual tribute.

270.   -47. The first monastery founded.

329.   -48. Constantine, emperor of Rome, removes the seat of empire to Byzantium, called, from his, Constantinople.

404.   -49. The kingdom of Caledonia, or Scotland, revives under Fergus. *Read page 15.*

420.   -50. Pharamond, the first king of France. *Read page 16.*

426.   -51. The Romans evacuate Britain. *Read page 16.*[1]

449.   -52. Archery first introduced into England; to which our ancestors owed their conquests.

457.   -53. Commencement of the Heptarchy, or Seven Kingdoms of the Saxons in England. *Go to No. 66.*

516.   -54. Dionsius, a monk, introduces the computation of time by the Christian era.

540.   -55. Knighthood instituted in England

555.   -56. The manufacture of silk introduced into Europe.

557.   -57. A dreadful plague all over Europe, Asia and Africa; which continued several years. *Stop one turn to deplore this calamity.*

570.   -58. Mahomet born. *Read in page 18.*

580.   -59. Latin ceased to be spoken in Italy about this time.

602. -60. The supremacy of the Pope established by the concession of Phocus, Emperor of the East.

604. -61. The first church of St Paul built in London, of wood, by Ethelbert.

622. -62. Death of Mahomet.

637. -63. Jerusalem taken by the Saracens.

653. -64. The Danes make their first appearance on the English coast. *See page 18.*

800. -65. Charlemagne, Emperor of the West.

827. -66. Egbert unites the kingdoms of the Saxon Heptarchy.

837. -67. Greenland discovered; and the whale fishery established by the Norwegians.

838. -68. The Picts totally defeated by the Scots, and both kingdoms united under Kenneth. *Pay 2 to your conquerors at No. 49.*

880. -69. The navy of England first established by Alfred. *Spin again.*

890. -70. Alfred the Great divides England into counties, etc. and defeats the Danes.

912. -71. Chivalry begins in England.

975. -72. Pope Boniface VII, deposed, and banished from Rome for his crimes. *Go back to No. 45.*

1000. -73. Paper, made of cotton rags, first used in England.

1002. -74. A great massacre of the Danes in England. *Pay 1 to Alfred, at No. 70.*

1015. -75. Children forbidden by the English law to be sold by their parents!

1066. -76. Battle of Hastings. *Say who was slain here, or pay 3 to the Pool.*

1080. -77. The Tower of London built by William the Conqueror, to overawe his English subjects.

1095. -78. The first crusade undertaken by several Christian princes. *Pay 2 to the Pool for its ill success.*

1150. -79. Chemistry, and distilling, introduced into Europe by the Moors.

1163. -80. London Bridge, consisting of 19 small arches, first built of stone.

1172. -81. Ireland conqueror by Henry II; since which it has been governed by an English viceroy, or lord lieutenant. *Pay 1 to No. 51.*

1180. -82. Glass windows first used in private houses in England.

1182. -83. The kings of France and England evince their submission to Pope Alexander III by holding the stirrups while he mounts his horse. *Pay 2 on No. 60.*

1190. -84. Geography brought into Europe by the Moors.

1215. -85. King John compelled by his barons to sign the Magna Charta. *Spin again.*

1273. -86. The empire of the House of Austria begins in Germany. *Read page 19.*

1280. -87. The mariner's compass invented.

1282. -88. Edward I defeats Llewellyn, Prince of Wales, and united that country to England. *Pay 1 to the conquerors at No. 51.*

1298. -89. Commencement of the present Turkish empire in Bythinia, under Othman. *Read page 20.*

1300. -90. Coal-mines discovered in Newcastle.

1315. -91. Establishment of the Helvetian Confederacy, or present Republic of Switzerland. *Pay 1 to No. 86, as, before this, it formed part of the dominions of Germany.*

1340. -92. Gunpowder invented by Swartz, a monk.

1340. -93. Oil-painting first practiced by Van Eyck.

1349. -94. Order of the Garter instituted.

1358. -95. France subdued by Edward III.

1362. -96. John Wickliffe exposes the errors of the Roman Church. *Spin again.*

1440. -97. The art of printing with metal types invented by John Guttenburg, at Strasburg. *Take 3 from the Pool.*

1446. -98. One hundred thousand people drowned by an irruption of the sea at Dort in Holland. *Stop one turn to lament this catastrophe.*

1460. -99. Engraving on copper invented.

1491. -100. The Moors expelled from Spain. *Read page 20.*

1492. -101. America first discovered by Columbus.

1497. -102. South America discovered by Americus Vesputius, after whom the whole continent was named.

1509. -103. Gardening introduced into England from the Netherlands, whence vegetables used to be imported.

1521. -104. Revolution in Sweden under Gustavus Vasa. *Read page 21.*

1522. -105. The first voyage round the world performed by a ship in Magellan's squadron.

1537. -106. Dissolution of religious houses in England. *Reward Wickliffe, at No. 96, with 1 counter.*

1564. -107. William Shakespeare born. *Receive 1 from each player to reward his genius.*

1572. -108. Massacre of St. Bartholomew at Paris, when 70,000 Protestants were butchered in cold blood. *Stop one turn.*

1582. -109. The New Style of calculation introduced by Pope Gregory, from whom it is called the Gregorian Style.

1588. -110. Destruction of the Spanish Armada. *Give some account of this, or pay 1, and read it on page 30.*

1649. -111. Charles I, king of England, beheaded at Whitehall.

1665. -112. Sixty-eight thousand persons destroyed by the plague in London. *Stop two turns.*

1666. -113. The great fire of London, which continued three days and consumed 13,000 houses. *Stop one turn.*

1693. -114. The first public lottery.

1701. -115. Prussia erected into a kingdom. *Read page 21.*

1704. -116. The Russian empire civilized by Peter the Great. *Read page 21.*

1710. -117. The present Cathedral of St. Paul built by Sir Christopher Wren.

1729. -118. Air-balloons invented by B. Gusman.

1749. -119. The ruins of Herculaneum discovered forty feet under ground.

1755. -120. Lisbon destroyed by an earthquake, and fifty thousand inhabitants killed.

1760. -121. Accession of George III to the throne of England. *Spin again.*

1764. -122. Longitude discovered by Harrison's time-piece.

1765. -123. South-sea islands discovered.

1775. -124. War between Great Britain and America. *Pay 1 to the Pool.*

1779. -125. Death of Captain Cooke at Owhyee. *Stop one turn to lament this great man.*

1784. -126. Mail-coaches first used in England.

1787. -127. Botony-Bay colonized with English convicts.

1789. -128. Destruction of the Bastile, and commencement of the French Revolution.

1793. -129. The King and Queen of France beheaded by the guillotine. *Pay 1 to No. 50.*

1795. -130. The kingdom of Poland annihilated, and divided between Germany, Russia and Prussia.

1799. -131. Seringapatam in India taken by the English.

1799. -132. Bonaparte elected Chief Counsul of France for ten years.

1802. -133. Two planets observed, called after their discoverers, Piazzi and Olbers.

1804. -134. Bonaparte crowned Emperor of the French by the Pope. *Pay 2 to No. 129.*

1806. -135. Taking of the Cape of Good Hope by the British.

1806. -136. Spain invaded by the French, and the Prince Regent of Portugal compelled to fly to his American dominions.

1812. -137. Ruinous expedition of Bonaparte to Moscow.

1812. -138. His Royal Highness George Prince of Wales created Regent of the British Empire. *You are appointed First Lord of the Treasury; therefore take possession of the Pool, with all the Counters on the board, and proclaim the Game at an end.*

1820. -139. His majesty George IV created king following the death of his father.

1833. -140. The abolition of colonial slavery during the reign of William IV.

1837. -141. Queen Victoria ascended the throne at the age of eighteen.

1840. -142. Marriage of Queen Victoria to Prince Albert of Saxe-Coburg and Gotha.

-143. *Complete your journey upon the railway, take possession of the Pool and proclaim the game at an end.*

This game illustrates what the publishers felt was important and what they were aware of in terms of scientific information. One interesting fact is that only one exclamation mark is used – No. 75, concerning the selling of children. Spelling has changed from the date of the game, for example verbs ending in '-ize' are now generally spelt '-ise' in England while retaining their original spelling in North America. The rules for the game are quite simple:

1. The materials for playing this game are, a Teetotum, four travellers, to show at which place each player stands in the Game; and one dozen counters for each, which may be pieces of card or any other substance. [This statement removed the element of using gaming counters, not desirable for children to be paying with.]
2. Let a traveller be given to each player.
3. Each player must put three counters into the pool.
4. Let the first player spin, and, placing his traveller on the Game according to the number turned up refer to the Chronology of Events, and observe the directions there given.
5. Whenever a player is directed to read the history of any event in another page, he shall have the privilege, after so doing, of spinning again, and be rewarded with a counter from each player.
6. The fines placed on any number are only to be taken by those who arrive at it by spinning; and not when sent from another number: neither are the directions to be observed.
7. If two persons arrive at the same number, the last comer shall return to his former place, and receive one from the first for so doing.
8. After the Game has gone once round, the first player is to spin again, and add that number which turns up to his former one. Thus, if he were at 8, and at his second spin turn up 6, he moves on to 14; and in this manner proceed till some one arrive at 143: but whoever goes beyond that must return to his former place, till some one arrive at the lucky number, who takes all the counters and wins the Game.

Reducing the period covered allowed the publishers to go into detail about the history that they and the buying public felt had determined their country. John Harris and John Wallis issued in 1803 *The Historical Pastime or New Game of the History of England with a Short Account of the Principal Events which have occurred from William the Conqueror to the Accession of George the Third*. Comprising 158 medallions or squares, in the spiral format it shows George III as the central image. The accompanying booklet sets out the reasons for the game and states, rather pompously, what they are hoping to achieve, always remembering that the children playing the game would be under the age of twelve:

ADVERTISEMENT
The utility and tendency of this Game must be obvious at first sight; for surly there cannot be a more agreeable study than History, and none more improving to Youth, than that which conveys to them, in a pleasing and comprehensive manner, the Events which have occurred in their own country.

The little Prints, which are regularly numbered from 1 to 158, represent either Portraits of the principal Personages who have signalised themselves as Kings, Statesmen, Churchman, Generals, Poets &c., &c. or some remarkable Occurrence in our country. – This will naturally excite a curiosity in the youthful mind; and that curiosity will be gratified in to short account of each reign subjoined. – On the whole, the writer flatters himself, that the public approbation will convince him, that the hours he has devoted to the formation of this little Scheme, have not been spent in vain.

RULES AND REGULATIONS FOR PLAYING
THE HISTORICAL GAME
This game comprehends nearly one hundred and sixty of the principal circumstances in the History of England, commencing with the Battle of Hastings and ending with

the Accession of George the Third, with appropriate Fines or Rewards, to most of the subjects. It is played with a tee-totum, numbered from 1 to 8. Each player proceeds in the Game according to the number he turns, and receives the Reward or pays the Fine appointed.

There are likewise twelve Letters, one of which each player must draw; and he who draws the earliest in the Alphabet, takes the privilege of turning first, and the others in rotation.

Each player must place his Letter on the circumstance to which he turns, to show his situation in the Game.

If any player turns to the subject on which another has his Letter, he takes that place and the other moves one forward, except at the Holy Land, where as many may be placed as chance may send.

Each player advances in the Game by adding the Figure that he turns to the Number on which his Letter stands.

Any number of persons may play; and he who arrives first at the Treasury, wins the Games, takes the Stakes and all forfeits that remain.

EXAMPLE

Suppose George, Charles and James play the Game, George draws B, Charles F, James H, they each put a stake into the Treasury. George having the earliest letter in the alphabet, spins first No. 3, places his Letter on the Briton, and pays a fine of one to the Norman. −Charles turns next No. 6, from which he derives no advantage, because every player must enter Doom's Day Book before he can proceed. − James next turns No. 4, takes the fine from the Norman, and passes to Doom's Day Book. − George then plays again, and turns No. 2, takes his letter from the Briton, and places it on Doom's Day Book; in consequence, James passes his Letter one forward, to the forest and pays a fine to the king.

As with the other games, this was reissued in 1828 with minor changes to show King George IV in a handsome scarlet jacket instead of the rather stylised profile of his father looking Roman in demeanour. Rather than having each illustration coloured, only four colours are used to handpaint the medallions.

In 1810, George III celebrated his jubilee and John Harris published a companion game entitled *The Jubilee, An Interesting Game* with a central image of the King in his robes, seated on the throne. In the booklet, he explained his reasons under the title 'Advertisement', however, it was singing the praises of the king. The rules of play, although similar, do have some major changes.

ADVERTISEMENT
This Game may be considered as a Continuation of one published a few years back, entitled HISTORICAL PASTIMES OF ENGLAND, which commenced at the Conquest and ended at the Accession of his present Majesty. where that left off, this begins; and it is hoped that the Events recorded (and surely an eventful Reign it has been) will create a lively interest in the breast of every Juvenile Briton; it is continued to the 25th of October 1809, the day our revered Sovereign entered the Fiftieth year of his Reign, and a Day of Jubilee in every part of his Dominions.

The writer of this has only to unite his wishes with those of his fellow subjects, that our good King may long continue to be the Ruler, as he has hitherto been the Father of a free and generous People.

RULES AND DIRECTIONS FOR PLAYING THE JUBILEE
In playing this Game, a teetotum of eight sides is made use of, together with six counters of different colours, as

markers, to avoid confusion in telling the game. Each player should also be provided with about two dozen of counters, on which a nominal value should be set, that any player who happens to be out, may purchase of the winners.

If more than six persons sit down to play, a greater number of markers may be cut out of card, and distinguished by figures, as may be agreed on.

Each player proceeds in the game according to the numbers he spins, and pays the fine, or receives the reward appointed. Advances are made by adding the figure turned to that on which the marker stands.

Should any player spin a number on which there is already a marker, he must take its place and the other must move one forward.

Any player taking more than his due, must go back as many numbers as he took. If he take too few, and the next player have spun, he must remain where he was.

Whatever fines are marked in the list of numbers, must be put into the pool, and the first who makes exactly 150, or 'The Jubilee' wins the game; but if he happens to spin above that number, he must go back as many from 150 as he spun beyond it, till he or some one else wins the pool and its contents.

Persons going backward in the game are exempted from the fines attached to the figures on which they be obliged to rest.

EXAMPLE

Suppose John, Thomas and James play the game; James chooses a white marker, Thomas a red and John a green one; James by agreement spins first; and finding the uppermost number of the teetotum to be 2, he places his Marker on the Funeral of George the Second. Thomas spins next, No. 8, and places his mark on the Birth of the Prince of Wales. John next turns No 1 and places his mark on the

Proclamation of George the Third. James then plays again, and spins No. 8 which being added to 2, his former number, sends him forward to the Commitment of Wilkes to the Tower, when he is to pay 2 counters to the pool, and go back to No. 1. Thomas spins No. 7 which, added to 8, his former number, brings him to the first meeting of the American Congress. John then spins No. 5, which added to 1, his former number, carries him to the Declaration of War against Spain and pays two counters to the Pool. Again James spins No. 5, which authorises him to take the station occupied by Thomas's mark. Thomas therefore moves to No. 16; and John having spun No. 3 moves to No. 9.

The overall text in this game praises the King in quite flowery language and also mentions scientific and geographical discoveries. However, it does not refrain from talking about the disagreeable events and laying the blame firmly on the King, especially for allowing the United States to rebel.

The game was adapted for the accession of George IV in 1820. Under the title *The Sun of Brunswick, a New and Interesting Game exhibiting the principal events during the reign of George the Good*, the centre image is the same as the one of George IV in the red jacket. The last few medallions have been reworked to show the death of Queen Charlotte, George III and Princess Charlotte of Wales together with Napoleon in exile, the Duke of Wellington and an Arctic expedition.

The last of the board games teaching history were published in the 1840s shortly after Queen Victoria came to the throne. *British Sovereigns*, published by Edward Wallis is a lavish game with only fifty-six squares. He started with Egbert in 827 and finished with the queen seated before a window with Windsor Castle in the background. Its rules of play are the same as other games except for one rules which states, 'If two players arrive at the same number, the one who arrived last must go back to his former number.'[2] Edward Wallis was at Skinner Street until 1847 when the premises and business was taken over by J. Passmore who reissued the game.

During the early part of the nineteenth century, England was not alone in publishing 'Historical Pastime', France too had a number of such games, all by the same publishers, Veuve Turgis, in the 1830s. *Jeu du Grand-Homme* looked at the life and times of Napoleon I, while *Jeu des Monuments de Paris* celebrated places of great interest. A further game, not strictly historical, was *Jeu des Cris de Paris,* about trades and businesses.

In 1791, C. Taylor published *An Arithmetic Pastime, intended to infuse the Rudiments of Arithmetic, under the idea of amusement.* A fairly plain game with a number of tables that every child should know – wine measures and avoirdupois, now known as pounds and ounces. Of course, many of the children playing these games were destined to become businessmen, solicitors and doctors so perhaps they needed these facts. Two teetotums were required for play, each numbered 0–9. Each player was furnished with a pyramid or marker and four counters of matching colours:

To learn addition:
Use but one teetotum, spin it and whatever number it turns up, move your traveller to the space so numbered. Let the other players do the same. When you spin it again, add your fresh number to your former one: thus if your former place was six and your fresh number 5, they together make 11, move there, spinning thus by turns, till one person gets 100. If a player's last spin carries him beyond 100, he does not win, but is to return as many on this side as he had got beyond; thus if his number would carry him to 108, that being 8 too many, he must return to 92, continuing so backwards and forwards, till someone hits the game exactly. Whenever a player comes to a picture, he must look at the list, to see how to proceed. When told to stop 1, 2, or 3 turns, he must put down so many

counters, and when his turn comes, instead of spinning, he must take one up.

To learn subtraction:
The general rules of the game are as before, only both tee-totums are to be spun. Two numbers will then arise, take the least from the greatest, and move with the remainder. If for instance, the numbers 7 and 4, subtract 4 from 7 and 3 remains, to number 3 you must go; if the next 9 and 5 arise, subtract and 4 remains, which added to you former place brings you to 7.

To learn multiplication:

Multiply the two numbers which arise, move with the last figure of their product, neglecting the other: thus if 5 and 9 appear, multiplied they make 45 – use the 5 and neglect the 4.

To learn division:
Divide the greatest number which come us by the least, observe how many times the latter is contained in the former and how many remain, add these together and move with their sum. Five and eight are contained one and 3 over; 3 and 1 is 4, move there.

There are twenty-one compartments containing pictures, such as a cake, tiger, sentry, peacock and a sheet of rules, which has a list of the penalties or benefits to be gained by a player who lands on a picture. This game not only taught arithmetic but also history, geography and morals. Later John Wallis issued the game and it was reissued for some years.

The subject of science sometimes mixed fact and fiction. This was well documented in a game first published by John Wallis in 1804 and then reissued by his son, Edward, entitled *Science in Sport, or the Pleasures of Astronomy, A New and Instructive Pastime. Revised and Approved by Mrs. Bryan,*

Blackheath. No indication is given about Mrs Bryan but as her location was Blackheath, she may have had dealings with the Royal Observatory at Greenwich.

The thirty-five squares have portraits of astronomers and show astronomical phenomena, the movements of the planets, comets and rainbows intermingled with signs of the Zodiac and the Man in the Moon. It also attempted to teach some moral behaviour, especially studying.[3]

It is in the game *The Circle of Knowledge, A New Game of the Wonders of Nature, Science and Art* where fact and fiction are totally amalgamated. The board is marked with four concentric circles and divided into sixteen subjects each with three compartments leading to either a sign of the Zodiac or one of the cardinal points of the compass. The subjects covered include continents – Europe, Asia, Africa and America, the four seasons, four sciences – electricity, chemistry, optics and astronomy, and finish with earth, air, fire and water.

The illustrations are varied and unusual, for example Spring is shown as dancing round a maypole, a rainbow and birds feeding their young, while Air is a balloon and parachute, a shipwreck and a windmill. The Science subjects reflect new and old ideas as Chemistry shows an alchemist, a scientific lecture and a chemist's shop and the Optics a telescope, perspective down a tunnel and a magic lantern. It is the Fire that is the violent one with a volcano, burning buildings and a pit explosion.

Players would progress round the game on the spin of a teetotum or the selection of a numbered card. At each stop, they would be required to describe the events happening in the illustration and it is possible that forfeits and rewards would be given depending on each. It is possible to give forfeits and rewards to each square and some are more obvious than others, such as a fire or a shipwreck signalling to go backwards or perhaps start again. The game was published by John Passmore in the 1840s.

Natural history was not forgotten, especially as many new and varied animals were found during explorations around the world. *British and Foreign Animals, A New Game, Moral, Instructive, and Amusing, designed to allure the Minds of Youth to an Acquaintance with the Wonders of Nature* actually does keep to facts even though the publisher, William Darton, did overdo his desire to instruct children. One must always remember that the games were designed for children under the age of twelve. Their language and reading abilities had to be good but reading about some of the animals may have put them off, as shown in the text for the Jackal.

THE JACKAL

In the torrid regions of Africa and Asia, these active and rapacious beasts supply the place which is occupied in temperate and frozen districts by the wolf. The hotter the climate, the greater is their strength and vigour. They collect together, and hunt their prey, in packs of from forty to fifty in number, and attack and devour all kinds of animals. In the burning plains of Egypt and Arabia, they follow the caravans, for the purpose of feeding on whatever is left behind. The lion and the panther oftentimes lurk in the rear of the jackals, and as often rob them of at least part of their prey; hence appears to have arisen the erroneous notion of the Jackal being the lion's provider. These animals live in burrows, which they dig under the surface of the ground; and from which they seldom issue, except during the stillness of the night. Their howling, when in pursuit of prey, is said to be dreadful. If caught young, they may be rendered perfectly tame and domestic. Like a dog, they distinguish their master from every other person, eat out of his hand, and love to be fondled and patted. In many respects the jackal has a great resemblance to the fox. Although it is one of the most numerous of all the wild animals of the East, there is scarcely any one less known in Europe, or more confusedly described by natural historians. They vary in size. Those of the warmest climates are said to be the largest. Nothing can escape their rapacity. They will ransack the repositories of the dead, and greedily devour the most putrid bodies. They are said to attend caravans and to follow armies, in hopes of being furnished with a banquet by disease or battle. They may be considered as the vulture among quadrupeds; and like that destructive bird, devour every thing indiscriminately that once had animal life.

The descriptions follow in like manner and many of the illustrations order movement with in the game. Some of these are handwritten (those marked ★).

1. THE JACKAL.
2. THE COMMON OTTER, SPIN AGAIN.★
3. THE DORMOUSE, LEST THE PLAYER SLEEP OVER THIS DROWSY ANIMALS, LET HIM PASS TO NO. 35.
4. THE SIX BANDED ARMADILLO. STOP ONE TURN.★
5. THE ZEBRA.
6. THE FERRET.
7. THE RABBIT. STOP ONE TURN.
8. THE HEDGEHOG. GO ON TO NO. 16.★
9. THE BEAVER. HERE STOP ONE TURN, TO EXAMINE THE CURIOUS HABITATIONS DESCRIBED.
10. THE HARE. SPIN AGAIN.★
11. THE SHEEP. STOP ONE TURN.★
12. THE RAT.
13. THE BULL. STOP TWO TURNS.
14. THE HORSE. SPIN AGAIN, FOR A RIDE ON ONE OF THESE NOBLE ANIMALS.
15. THE CAMEL. GO ON TO NO. 20.★
16. THE ELK. STOP ONE TURN.★

17. THE ELEPHANT. SPIN AGAIN.★
18. THE PORCUPINE. STOP ONE TURN TO REFRESH.
19. THE HYAENA.
20. THE WILD BOAR. STOP ONE TURN, TO TAKE BREATH AFTER THE DANGEROUS HUNT.
21. THE LYNX. GO BACK ONE TURN LEST THE PIERCING EYE OF THIS ANIMAL DISCOVER YOUR FOIBLES.
22. THE POINTER. MOVE ON TO 26.★
23. THE SOW.
24. THE RACOON. BEGIN AGAIN.★
25. THE MONKEY. MOVE ON TO NO. 31 AND SEE WHICH YOU LIKE BEST.
26. THE ASS. SPIN AGAIN.★
27. THE STAG. STOP ONE TURN.★
28. THE CAT. STOP ONE TURN TO ADMIRE BLACK TOM.★
29. THE IBEX.
30. THE GUINEA PIG.
31. THE BABOON.
32. THE FOX. STOP TWO TURNS TO ELUDE THE TRICKS OF THIS WILY ANIMAL.
33. THE GOAT.
34. THE JERBOA. STOP ONE TURN.★
35. THE SQUIRREL.
36. THE KANGAROO. GO BACK TO 26.★
37. THE LION.

The game starts with the Jackal and ends with the Lion. Much compassion is shown for this animal, which is described as fierce and already on the verge of extinction.[4] There are some intriguing animals included when you consider that Darton published this in 1820. There is a kangaroo, an armadillo, beaver, ibex and lynx among the thirty-seven described.

Morals

What better way to teach moral and good behaviour than a game that encourages winning and gambling. The Protestant publishers found that games could be influential and a well-designed and well-thought-out game very successful. The best-known one, perhaps because of its title, is *The New Game of Virtue Rewarded and Vice Punished, for the Amusement of Youth of Both Sexes*. It is quite firmly stated in the accompanying booklet the aims of the both the publisher, William Darton, and the author, Thomas Newton. 'IT IS DESIGNED WITH A VIEW TO PROMOTE THE PROGRESSIVE IMPROVEMENT OF THE JUVENILE MIND, AND TO DETER THEM FROM PURSUING THE DANGEROUS PATHS OF VICE.'

The rules for the game are much the same as any of the race games, however, the dice is marked 1 to 4, and any number of players to a maximum of twelve may partake. It is worth recording the various virtues and vices, and their rewards of forfeits, as it illustrates the feeling at the time of both the publishing world and the purchasing world.

DIRECTIONS

I.   House of Correction. Whoever gets into this must wait while every other player turns three times.

II.   Prudence. Is to have the privilege of turning again.

III.   Hypocrisy. Must forfeit two counters into the back and one to each player.

IV.   Honesty. Must receive one counter from each player.

V.   Folly. Must pay two counters into the back and turn again.

VI.   Charity. Is allowed to turn three times successively.

VII.   Avarice. Must forfeit half his counters into the bank.

VIII.   Poverty. Is to be relieved by two counters from the bank.

IX.   The Stocks. Whoever gets into the Stocks must wait whilst every other player turns twice.

X.   Faith. Claims one counter from each player.

XI.   Impertinence. Must go back to Prudence to learn good manners.

XII.   Truth. Must receive four counters from the bank and one from each player.

XIII.   Sloth. Must be sent to the House of Correction and wait while every other player turns twice.

XIV.   Hope. Must wait with patience until the next turn.

XV.   Luxury. Must pay one counter into the bank and one to each player.

XVI.   Friendship. Is to have the privilege of turning again.

XVII.   Carelessness. Must be sent back to Prudence.

XVIII.   Patience. Claims three counters from the bank.

XIX.	Brutality. Must be sent to the House of Correction.
XX.	Morality. Is to receive one counter from each player.
XXI.	Malice. Must pay one counter to each player and one into the bank.
XXII.	Modesty. Is entitled to turn again.
XXIII.	Contention. Must forfeit one counter to each player and turn again.
XXIV.	Piety. Is allowed to advance to Temperance.
XXV.	Envy. Must wait while every other player turns twice.
XXVI.	Confusion. Must go back to the number he last turned from.
XXVII.	Diligence. Must be rewarded with one counter from each player and turn again.
XXVIII.	Obstinacy. Must go back to Patience and pay two counters into the bank.
XXIX.	Civility. May advance two steps.
XXX.	Falsehood. Must be put in the Stocks while every player turns three times.
XXXI.	Temperance. Is allowed the privilege of turning again.
XXXII.	Anger. Must go back to Patience and remain while every player turns twice.
XXXIII.	Virtue. Claims the contents of the bank and wins the game.

The game, published in 1818, had thirty-three medallions around a flowery spiral with the titles marked on a ribbon-like band. The hand-coloured etching of twelve paper panels was mounted on linen. Thomas Newton also invented *The Mansion of Bliss, A New Game for the Amusement of Youth*. Less ornate, the titles are accompanied by a four-line verse that gives the rewards or penalties. The game was designed 'with a view to promote the progressive improvement of the juvenile mind and to deter them from pursuing the dangerous paths of vice'. The same virtues and vices are listed but they are much less theoretical and related directly to behaviour:

1. Innocent Amusement
2. Precipitation
3. Adversity
4. Bride well (prison)
5. Good Example
6. Negligent Shepherd
7. Brotherly Love
8. Herd of Swine
9. The Peace-Maker
10. Fighting
11. The School
12. Cruelty To Animals
13. Humanity
14. Robbing Orchards
15. Obedience to Parents
16. Prodigal Son
17. Repentant Prodigal
18. Taking Birds' Nests
19. Charity
20. The Truant
21. The Sailor
22. Swearing
23. The Blind Man
24. The Gamester
25. Fidelity
26. The Mimic
27. Purity
28. The Detractor
29. Filial Duty
30. Danger of Temptation

31. The Ship
32. False Friendship
33. The Disappointment
34. The Mansion of Bliss

Both games are similar to one published in 1804 by John Harris, *The New Game of Emulation designed for the Amusement of Youth of Both Sexes with an Abhorrence of Vice and a Love of Virtue*. At the opening of the booklet, called an Advertisement, the author states exactly what is expected to be learned by the players as they travel through the sixty-six virtues and vices.

ADVERTISEMENT
It is universally acknowledged that a spirit of emulation should be constantly encouraged in the rising generation, as the surest means of facilitating their progress in the paths of literature, and impressing their opening minds with the love of virtue. Youth are ever anxious for applause and remuneration, and will cheerfully exert themselves to obtain an honorary prize, even when admonitions and menaces prove unavailing. They are, also, perfectly aware of the consequences of disgrace, and naturally dread it, as the severest punishment.

Convinced of the truth of these observations, the author of the game now laid before the public, has endeavoured to instil into the minds of young people such sentiments as are most likely to conduce to their permanent felicity; for, whilst amusing themselves and their juvenile companions with their teetotum and counters, they will be led, almost imperceptibly, to admire and adopt the virtues of Obedience, Truth, Honesty, Gentleness, Industry, Frugality, Forgiveness, Carefulness, Mercy, and Humility; and to view in their real colours the opposite vices of Obstinacy, Falsehood, Robbery, Passion, Sloth,

Intemperance, Malice, Neglect, Cruelty and Pride. The other emblematical figures are calculated to render the game as interesting as possible, and will be found to conduce equally to the rational amusement and improvement of the mind.

For the first half of the nineteenth century, these moral games were published with fanciful titles, *The Mount of Knowledge*, *The Reward of Merit* and *The Cottage of Content or Right Road and Wrong Ways*. This last game, published by William Spooner about 1848, uses a teetotum with only four sides, marked F, R, L, B, (forward, right, left and back) and the roads are marked with forfeits and rewards. The direction shown on the teetotum is the one the player must follow. All start at the bottom and eventually arrive at *The Cottage of Content*[1] at the top.

A development from the strictly moral interpretation was a game of life, showing the growth of a person from infancy to old age and death. Throughout the path, the person struggles with his own good and bad behaviour. *The New Game of Human Life, with Rules for Playing being the Most Agreeable and Rational Recreation ever Invented for Youth of Both Sexes,* was published by John Wallis and Elizabeth Newbery in 1790. It has the instructions to use a teetotum to avoid introducing a dice box to a private family. The rules and explanations cover all the area of the printed sheets that are not occupied by the playing surface. This is a flattened spiral, numbered one to eighty-four. In the centre under the title are 'The Rules of the Game'.

The Immortal Man, who has existed 84 years, seems worthy of his Talents and Merit to become for the Close of Life, which can end only by Eternity. When we shall arrive at the No.84, we shall have gain'd all we can by this Game, but if we exceed this number, we must go back as many points as we have proceeded beyond it.

The Age of Man is divided into seven periods of 12 years, viz. Infancy to Youth, Manhood, Prime of Life, Sedate Middle Age, Old Age, Decrepitude and Dotage. He passes through life in a variety of situations which are arranged in the order they generally succeed each other.

This game like all others of the same kind is played with a totum, each Player spinning twice in his turn, the only difference is, that the Players cannot stop at any one of the seven ages, but must proceed as many points beyond, as they have in coming to them. Yet as they may spin at the first 2 sixes and consequently would go onto 84, which would be most improper, those who have this chance at first, must content them selves with going to the Historian at 39.

The Studious Boy at 7 shall receive a Stake and shall proceed to 42, the place of the Orator.

The Negligent Boy at 11 shall pay a Stake and shall remain two rounds without spinning.

The Assiduous Youth at 15 shall receive 2 Stakes, and proceed to 55, where he will find the Patriot.

The Triflet at 19 shall pay 1 Stake, and proceed to the Songster at 38.

The Duellist at 22 shall pay 2 Stakes, and return to take the place of the Boy at Number 3.

The Complaisant Man at 26 shall remain there, and let others play until another comes to take his place, and then he shall go back to the place of his liberator.

The Prodigal at Number 30 shall pay four Stakes, and go back to the Careless Boy at Number 6.

The Married Man at 34 shall receive two Stakes for his Wife's Portion and go to be a Good Father at 56.

The Romance Writer at 40 shall pay 2 Stakes and go back to the Mischievous Boy at 5.

The Dramatist at 44 shall pay 4 Stars to the Masters of his Art and shall begin the game again.

The Benevolent Man at 52 shall go to 78 to amuse himself with the Joker.

The Temperate Man at 58 shall go to 82, to find the Quiet Man.

The Drunkard at 63 shall pay 2 Stakes and go back to the Child at 2.

The Patient Man at 68 shall receive 2 Stakes and go to amuse himself with the merry fellow at 80.

The Manhater at 71 shall pay 2 Stakes and go back to the Obstinate Youth at 16.

The Old Beau at 74 shall receive 1 Stake and let each of the others play one round.

The Satyrist at 77 shall pay 4 Stakes and go back to the Malignant Boy at 8.

Lastly the Tragic Author at 45 shall go to the place of the Immortal Man at 84 and win the Game by Succeeding him.

In each of the four spandrels further directions and explanations are given:

1. The Utility and Moral Tendency of this Games. If parents who take upon themselves the pleasing task of instructing their children (or others to whom that important trust may be delegated) will cause them to stop at each character and request their attention to a few moral and judicious observations, explanatory of each character as they proceed and contrast the happiness of a virtuous and well spent life with the fatal consequences arising from vicious and immoral pursuits, this game may be rendered the most useful and amusing of any that has hitherto been offered to the public.
2. Directions for Playing. This game may be played by any number of persons at a time; but care must be taken, that each player makes use of a different mark to move with, and be provided with at least twelve counters each, and agree how much to value them per dozen.

Let us then suppose that four gentlemen agree to play a game together, and stake four counters each. A takes red for his mark, B green, C black and D white. A begins and spins 9 and accordingly places his mark upon No. 9, which is the Docile Boy. B plays next and spins 7, but as the rules of the game specify instead of putting his mark on No.7, he must receive a counter from the pool, and carry his mark to the Orator, at No. 42. C being next in turn, spins only 2, and puts his mark on the place of the Child at No. 2. D being the last player spins 11, and goes to the Negligent Boy; but this being a forfeit, he must pay a counter to the pool and remain two rounds at No. 11 without playing in his turn. A now resumes the totum and spins 3, which brings him from No. 9 where he was to No. 12, but this being one of the seven ages, he cannot stop there, for agreeable to the rules of the game he must proceed as far beyond the age to No. 15, the place of the Assidious Youth; but instead of that he must receive 2 counters from the pool and go to No. 55, the place of the Patriot. B now takes the totum and spins 6, when being already at No. 42, the place of the Orator, he should naturally go to No. 48 but that being the age of the Sedate Man, he must proceed 6 points beyond 48 and put his mark on the place of the Vigilant Man at no 54. C's turn being but instead of stopping at this last number (according to the rules of the game) he pays a counter into the pool and goes to the place of the Songster at No. 38. D must as already mentioned also remain this round without playing. A again takes the totum and spins 2, and being before at No. 82 compleats No. 84, takes the place of the Immortal Man and wins the game.

NB. It is necessary to inform the Purchaser the Totum must be marked with the figures 1–6 and avoid introducing a dice box into private families, each player must spin twice, which will answer the same purpose.

The playing surface is numbered in an anti-clockwise direction and the titles are as one would expect but not everyone is a dramatist, a romance writer, or even a coxcomb proud of his appearance. The full list follows:

1. The Infant; 2. The Child; 3. The Boy; 4. The Darling; 5. The Mischievous Boy; 6. The Careless Boy; 7. The Studious Boy; 8. The Malignant Boy; 9. The Docile Boy; 10. The Thoughtless Boy; 11. The Negligent Boy; 12. The Youth; 13. The Volunteer; 14. The Indolent Youth; 15. The Assiduous Youth; 16. The Obstinate Youth; 17. The Rebellious Youth; 18. The Gallant; 19. The Trifler; 20. The Lover; 21. The Idler; 22. The Duellist; 23. The Dissembler; 24. The Young Man; 25. The Decisive Man; 26. The Complaisant Man; 27. The Downright Man; 28. The Flatterer; 29. The Critic; 30. The Prodigal; 31. The Coxcomb; 32. The Generous Man; 33. The Economist; 34. The Married Man; 35. The Batchelor; 36. The Prime of Life; 37. The Author; 38. The Composer; 39. The Historian; 40. The Romance Writer; 41. The Poet; 42. The Orator; 43. The Comic Author; 44. The Dramatist; 45. The Tragic Author; 46. The Traveller; 47. The Geographer; 48. The Sedate Man; 49. The Imperious Man; 50. The Affable Man; 51. The Morose Man; 52. The Benevolent Man; 53. The Insensible Man; 54. The Vigilant Man; 55. The Patriot; 56. The Good Father; 57. The Ambitious Man; 58. The Temperate Man; 59. The Glutton; 60. The Old Man; 61. The Libertine; 62. The Philosopher; 63. The Drunkard; 64. The Miser; 65. The Gambler; 66. The Learned Man; 67. The Brute; 68. The Patient Man; 69. The Vindictive Man; 70. The Friend of Man; 71. The Man Hater; 72. Decrepitude; 73. The Sloven; 74. The Old Beau; 75. The Hasty Man; 76. The Hypochondriac; 77. The Satyrist; 78. The Joker; 79. The Silent Man; 80. The Merry Fellow; 81. The

Troublesome Companion; 82. The Quiet Man; 83. The
Thoughtful Man; 84. The Immortal Man.

The games of morals and behaviour spawned the greatest
number of copies by both European and American publishers. *La Vie Humaine, Un Nouveau Jeu*, published about 1800
by Simon Schropp in Berlin, despite its French title, bears
the reverse images of Wallis' game except for the last square.
Printed on silk rather than paper, it commemorates the life
and death of a leading figure, probably Leopold, Prince of
Brunswick (1752–85). In common with the majority of games
published in Germany all the titles are in four languages –
French, German, English and Polish – although sometimes
Italian is substituted for the Polish.

The game *The Mansion of Happiness* gives no indication by
its title of just how harsh its penalties were in comparison
to other moral games of its time. The crimes were serious
– theft, lying, cheating and drunkenness – with penalties
that included prison, whipping and the stocks. One penalty
was the ducking stool as illustrated by 'Whoever gets into a
Passion must be taken to the Water, have a ducking to cool
him and pay a fine of one'.

The game is unusual too because it gives an inventor's name,
a rare occurrence at this date of publication. George Fox, within
a year, 'invented' another game for a different publisher. *The
Mansion of Happiness* is a hand-coloured engraving published by
Robert Laurie and James Whittle in October 1800. It has sixty-
seven compartments, which represent various virtues and vices
together with, in the centre (sixty-seven) a view of Oaklands
Park. Under the central compartment is an eight-line verse
about vice and virtue. The publishers dedicated the game to the
Duchess of York, 1800, and the Mansion of Happiness is a representation of Oaklands Park, the residence of the Duke of York.

The 1843 American version of *The Mansion of Happiness, An
Instructive, Moral and Entertaining Amusement* is often classified

as the first of its kind. However, publishers had been producing geographical games from the 1820s. It is likely that the moral game was one of the first to be mounted on cardboard as opposed to the linen. W. & S.B. Ives published a number of board and card games. This particular game bears reverse impressions of the illustrations although the design of the game is quite different from the original published by Robert Laurie and James Whittle in 1800.

About 1825, Edward Wallis published *Every Man to His Station, A New Game*, which shows scenes of everyday life and in the centre boys actually playing the game with a teetotum. The game starts with the House of Correction and the majority of the game shows various evil traits and landing on such a square requires forfeits of payment of counters and missing turns. Working hard and being kind are the rewarded traits.

RULES FOR PLAYING
This game is played with a teetotum, bearing six faces and marked 1, 2, 3, 4, 5, 6 and many may join in the amusement.

Each player must be provided with ten counters and a traveller; each traveller varying in colour, that every player may know their own.

Before they begin, each player must deposit three counters into the bank.

When it has been agreed who shall begin the game, the first person, having spun the teetotum, must place his traveller upon the number corresponding with that which the teetotum presents uppermost. If a 1 turn up, he must place his traveller upon HOUSE OF CORRECTION, which the rule in the verse directs him to remain there while every other player turns the teetotum two times. If he should turn up 2, he must take his traveller there, which will be THE FERRYMAN, which verse directs him to turn the teetotum once more. And when it is his turn to spin again, he counts from the figure which bore his traveller last.

If any player be sent back, he must not act according to the direction of that figure: he must only go by the directions of the figure he last spun from; nor must he, if he be directed to advance to any figure, act according to the directions of that figure; but must only go by the directions of the figure he last spun from. The exception is the HOUSE OF CORRECTION where its rules must be obeyed.

If any player should turn up a number which would carry him beyond No. 33, THE WINNER, as many numbers as he turns beyond it, so many must he place his traveller back from the figure he spun from; viz. if his traveller be on THE WINDMILL, and he should spin a 3, he then will have spun 1 beyond the game; therefore he must place his traveller back upon THE RACE, which is 1 behind the figure he turned from, where he must remain till his turn comes again.

If two players arrive at the same number, the one who arrived first must go back to the second's former number. Should any player lose their counters, they must retire from the game.

NB As every symbol subjects the player to certain fines, rewards or removals, a thorough knowledge of their meaning, and the rules, must be acquired; and this may be done with even a moderate share of attention. At each spin, the player should read out the verse or instruction given; to shorten the game, it is permissible to follow the short instructions only.

1. HOUSE OF CORRECTION
Whoever gets into this must wait while every other player turns two times.
Well begun is half ended, but you've begun badly,
So enter your prison, where you'll be used sadly,

Stop twice while the others go on in their race,
When you're out, you'll endeavour to mend your slow pace.

Reflect when you enter this place;
For here none but the guilty are found;
While the rest of the play'rs turn twice,
In confinement you are to be bound.

2. THE FERRYMAN

For his act of Charity, he is allowed to turn one time in succession and receive a counter from every player.

Whoever relieves the distress'd,
Rewarded they surely must be,
With a counter from every play'r,
And turn once the teetotum with glee.

3. THE HOUSE

The Repentant Prodigal may receive two counters from the bank.

Thou'rt welcome again in this home,
I felt for and pitied thy fate;
Two counters receive from the Bank,
I'm glad thou return's not too late.

4. THE REAPER

As a reward for his Industry, he receives one counter from the bank and may proceed to No. 15, the Reaped Field.

All those who their parents assist,
When unable to toil any more,
Shall move forward again,
And receive from the Bank one counter more.

5. THE FATHER

The Father watches over the child and his love allows another spin.

We joy to see the op'ning bud,
It promises a lovely flow'r;
Joy swells the parent like a flood,
Whilst thee it watches every hour,
In hopes you will reward his love,
And grant you now a double move.

6. THE TRAVELLER

For his lazy and slothful behaviour, he must be carried back to the House of Correction and be confined for two spins and read the second verse.

The Prodigal son must go back
To wait on the swine in the field
Impudence has brought him to this
To which he now humbly must yield.

7. THE WOUNDED MAN

To learn from his Folly, he must wait until all the other players have spun once.

If prudence and wisdom you'd sought,
Your destruction you would not have found;
You here for your folly must stay,
While the rest turn the teetotum once round.

8. THE COWS

The animals must be driven forward to the Farmer's Wife, No. 16.

9. THE BROKEN BRIDGE

To overcome Disappointment and Adversity, return to the Charity of the Ferryman for passage, No. 2, but do not take advantage of the double spin.

Retrace now the steps whence you came,
O'er the bridge you now cannot proceed;
The way to it's difficult, indeed.

With patience adversity bear
Keep your mind from anxiety free;
So wait till your turn comes again,
And your fate may more fortunate be.

10. THE WATCHMAN
Whoever falls into his hands must be conducted to the House of Correction and abide by the governing rules.

11. THE BEGGAR
To cope with Poverty, receive two counters from the bank.

12. THE SMUGGLER
Smuggling shall make restitution of three counters to the bank and be sent to the House of Correction and abide by its rules.
To the House of Correction you must repair,
Smuggling is a crime, beyond doubt;
The teetotum twice round shall be spun,
After which you'll have leave to come out.

13. THE CRIPPLE
The needy our protection require so each player must a counter give; for none but the worthless refuse a poor being like this to relieve.
Since none but the good are found here,
Where love and humanity reign;
Claim a counter from every play'r.
Then wait till your turn come again.

14. THE CUSTONS HOUSE
Regularity and justice shall receive one counter from each player.
Fidelity's truly display'd
By the emblem of constancy here;

For your choice a counter demand,
Politely, from every player.

15. THE REAPED FIELD
The lazy one sleeps; he must return to the Reaper and wait till everyone spins again.
The lazy to the Reaper must return,
For such negligence cannot be look'd o'er;
And stay while each player turns twice,
Then, perhaps, he'll be guilty no more.

16. THE FARMER'S WIFE
Modesty; turn again and take a counter from each player.
With firmness temptation avoid,
As the sensitive plant doth the hand;
The teetotum again you may turn,
But a counter from each first demand.

17. THE HUNTSMAN
To learn his lesson about cruelty to animals, he shall pay one counter to the bank and begin the game again.
Who joins in this sport shall repent,
They the game shall begin o'er again;
For who, but a brute would rejoice,
To behold the poor beast in such pain.

18. THE VOLUNTEER
Your life you hazard for your country so move on to the Battle at No. 27.
The soldier may go to his ranks,
The Bulwark of this happy isle;
And from his position a leap take
For his bravery, danger and toil.

19. THE HERDSMAN
The negligent herdsman must pay two counters into the bank.
When the shepherd is e'er found alone,
To the bank he two counters must pay;
Then in future with care he'll attend,
That the flock can no more go astray.

20. THE PLOUGHMAN
You labour hard and scorn to grieve, so travel to No. 28
you receive.

21. THE INN
To partake of refreshments, pay one counter to the bank
and stay a time until every other player has spun once.

22. CUSTOMS OFFICER
The Danger of Temptation must be fought, so return to
your previous point.
Base bribes you must always avoid,
Or you'll perish before you're aware,
Retrace your steps whence you came,
And, in future, proceed with rare care.

23. THE HUNT
More haste may be less speed, so with care spin once.
Come, get up and ride, you're impatient to run;
Next time 'tis your turn, take two spins to their one.
If you should o'er shoot you'll repent, so take heed,
Or you'll make with your hurry more haste than good speed.

24. FALLEN JOCKEY
Pride's painful and comes before a fall,
Thus pay a counter out to one player and all.

25. THE MILLER

Resting after toil may not be enjoyed, but stop one turn will all others play.

Stop a turn here and rest you, you've come a long way;
If the hind'rance displeases, though only in play,
Then at work against hind'rance your watchfulness double,
For the loss then is real, and more weighty the trouble.

26. THE HORSE AND MASTER

Gentleness shall advance three steps to the Stables, No. 29.

27. THE BATTLE

Stand fast on the field of battle until a replacement comes to relieve you. If no replacement arrives after all others have spun twice, you may pay two to the bank to escape.

Come stand and do duty, no more from this place,
Till another arrives here, the station to grace;
If none should relieve you, all's lost, for 'tis clear,
You will ne'er reach the end, if you keep standing here.

28. THE PLOUGHED FIELD

Hard work is repaid by two counters for the bank.

Diligence and hard work what sight,
Is more pleasing than this;
Take two from the Bank and retire
For the night.

29. THE STABLES

Whoever is so unfortunate as to fall upon this number, loses his place in the game and must start again.

30. THE RACE

To learn from gaming losses he must return to the Jockey, No. 24.

A gamester the horses detest,
He, the innocent, strives to deceive,
And a return to the Jockey he pays.

31. THE WINDMILL
The sails are still, so stay until another your place takes.
However hard you think your case,
Stay here till some one take your place.
If some one should happ'n along to relieve,
Be thankful for such a reprieve.

32. THE RICHES
From your gains, pay each other player a counter and return to your previous place.
To take ill-gotten gains retrace
Then your steps whence you came
And a counter to each you are fined
To shun disappointment and shame
And not be stopt when almost at the end of your game.

33. THE WINNER
To the winner the spoils, take the bank as your prize and be first if another game is to be played.
Here's the end of your Labours, your hope and fear now,
May be the laurel of victory sit well on your brow.
As you've won, to rejoice is but natural and right.
But don't be insulting, and triumph with spite;
You might have been loser, may next, to your shame;
'Twas chance, and not merit, procured you the game.
One grain of good nature, self boasting to cheek,
Will far more than laurel, or diamond, deck,
He only deserves fair prosperity's smile,
Who, losing or winning, keeps temper the while.

By the middle of the nineteenth century, games based on teaching morals had all but disappeared in England. A number continued to be reissued in the United States. These games were replaced by others, in particular, *Snakes and Ladders*, which continued to stress good and bad but were perhaps more interesting to play. *Snakes and Ladders* was also a short game. Sometimes the early games, because of the forfeits or penalties, proved to be long games and occasionally a time limit was set for playing them.

1. A game of *Tag*.

2. *Blind Man's Bluff.*

Left: 3. Three-legged race.

Below: 4. Sack race.

5. Victorian Greetings Card showing children playing a game similar to *London Bridge is Falling Down*.

6. *Hop scotch*.

7. *Leap frog.*

8. Single skipping.

9. *Hula Hoop.*

10. *Whipping Top.* Illustrated on a child's pewter dish that has letters of the alphabet around the outer edge. American, 1890–1910.

11. *Hobby horse.*

12. *Diabolo.*

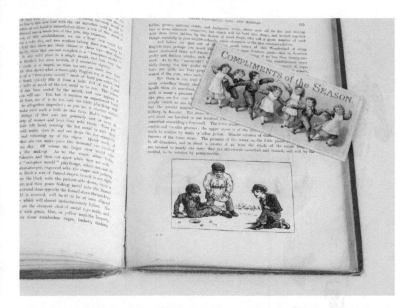

13. Playing a game of marbles. Illustration from *Wonderland of Work*, published by Cassell, Petter, Galpin & Co., about 1880.

14. Young women playing *Knucklebones*. Made of terracotta; said to be have been from Capua and made in Campania or Puglia, southern Italy; Hellenistic Greek, 330–300 BC.

15. *Stilts*.

16. Flying a kite.

17. *Piñata*.

18. *Solitaire* board. Turned wood and glass marbles, English, 2004.

19. *Tangram.*
Polished wood.

20. *Giant Dominoes.* Hand-finished wood; designed by Justine Cardy and made by Garden Games Limited; English, 2004.

21. *Noughts and Crosses*. Wood, designed and made by Jacques & Co. Ltd, 2006.

22. *Nine Men's Morris*. Polished and stained wood, made by James Masters.

23. *Giant Connect 4*. Plastic, designed by Justine Cardy and made by Garden Games Ltd, English, 2005. A large-scale wooden version of the game BIG 4 is also available but it is more suitable for indoor use.

24. *Balance Game*. Turned and painted wood, with a die marked in colours rather than spots.

25. *Chinese Checkers*. Turned wood with glass marbles, English, 2004.

26. *Halma*, set for two players. Polished and painted wood, made by James Masters.

27. *Halma*, set for four players. Polished and painted wood, made by James Masters.

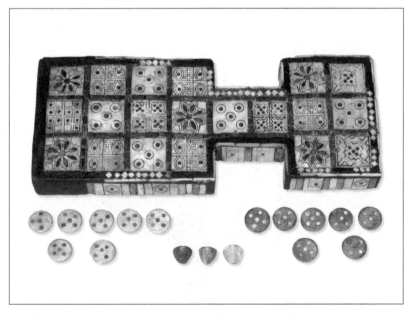

28. *The Royal Game of Ur.* Made of shell, red limestone and lapis lazuli over a wooden base. Ur, Southern Iraq, 2600–2400 BC.

29. Game of *Senet*. New Kingdom, Egypt, 1550–1069 BC.

30. Satirical scene of animals playing *Senet*. Papyrus, possibly from Thebes, late New Kingdom Egypt, about 1100 BC. The scene is from a document satirising Egyptian society.

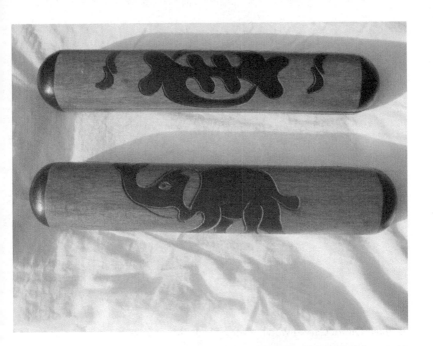

33. *Pencil Oware*, closed. Carved and stained wood, made by James Masters, 2006. By having the game in this form it may be carried around by a player from place to place and of course, player to player.

34. *Pencil Oware,* open. Carved and stained wood, made by James Masters, 2006.

Opposite above: 31. Spiral race game, possibly a board for *Mehen*. Limestone, Egypt, early Dynastic period.

Opposite below: 32. *Backgammon.* Wood, made by Jacques & Co. Ltd, 2006.

35. *Table Owari*. Carved wood, made by James Masters, 2006.

36. *Go*. Polished wood with slate and clamshell playing piece, made by James Masters, English, 2006.

Above: 37. *Go.* Close-up of the board showing the placement of the pieces on the lines and not within the squares.

Right: 38. *Il Gioco Dell'oca.* *DILET = TEVOLE per chi gioco e chi non gioco* (The Pleasing Game of Goose) Si Vendono Grana 5 Presso A Rosso a S Biaso n. 107. Published in Italy about 1750.

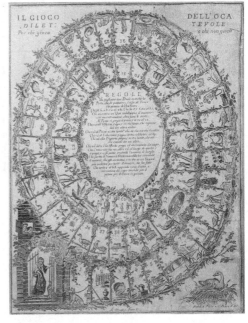

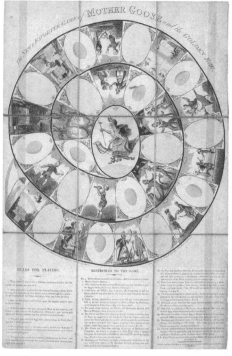

Above: 39. *Nouveau Jeu de L'oie.*[1]
Hand-coloured engraving
mounted on card, French, about
1850.[2]

Left: 40. *The New and Favourite
Game of Mother Goose and the
Golden Egg.*[3] Published and sold
wholesale by, John Wallis Sr,
13 Warwick Square and retail by
John Wallis Jr, 188 The Strand,
London, 13 November 1808.

41. *Dice*. Made of pewter in the style of dice hammered from lead musket balls by soldiers in the field so they may play dice games. American, 2006.

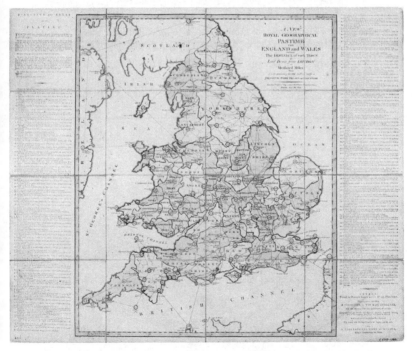

42. *A New Royal Geographical Pastime for England and Wales*. 'Whereby the Distance of each Town is laid down from London in measured miles being a very amusing game to play with a teetotum, ivory pillars and counters.' Published by Robert Sayer, No. 53 Fleet Street, London, 1 June 1787.

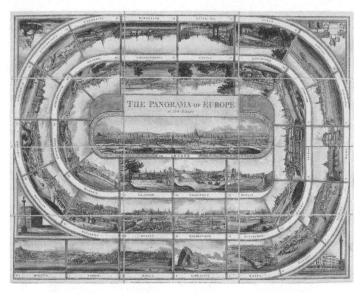

Above: 43. *The Panorama of Europe, A New Game.* Published by
J. & E. Wallis, 42 Skinner Street, London and I. Wallis Jr. Marine
Library, Sidmouth, Devon, 1 November 1815.

45. *A Tour Through the British Colonies and Foreign Possessions and Dioramic Game of the Overland Route to India.* Published by The Historical Games Company as a replica of the original game, English, 1994.

46. *The Noble Game of Elephant and Castle or Travelling in Asia.* Published by The Historical Games Company as a replica of the original game, English, 1994.

Opposite below: 44. Walker's New Geographical Game Exhibiting a Tour Through Europe. Published for the author and sold by W. & T. Darton, Holborn Hill, London, 1 May 1810.

47. *Wallis's New Game of Universal History and Chronology*. Published by The Historical Games Company as a replica of the original game, English, 1994.

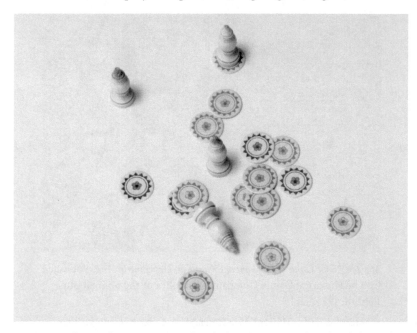

48. Die, markers and counters. Issued with the new game and made of plastic representing bone.

49. *Historical Pastime, A New Game of the History of England*. Published by Edward Wallis, No. 42 Skinner Street and J. Harris & Son, St Paul's Churchyard, London, in 1828.

50. *British Sovereigns*. Published by Edward Wallis, 42 Skinner Street, London about 1840.

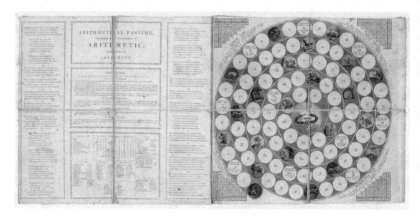

51. *An Arithmetical Pastime*, intended to infuse the rudiments of arithmetic, under the idea of amusement. Published by C. Taylor and later by John Wallis; Printed by Biggs & Co., Crane Court, Fleet Street for John Wallis, 16 Ludgate Street, London, 1791 and 1798.

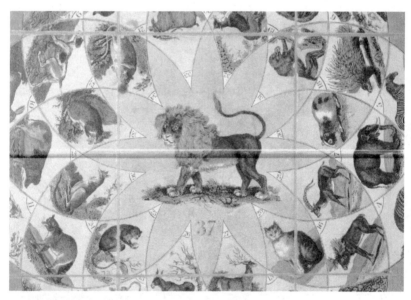

52. *British and Foreign Animals, a New Game, Moral, Instructive, and Amusing*, designed to allure the minds of youth to an acquaintance with the wonders of nature; originally published by William Darton, 58 Holborn Hill, London, 1820. Published by The Historical Games Company as a replica of the original game, English, 1994.

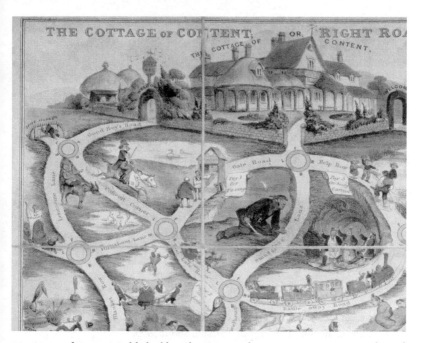

53. *Cottage of Content*. Published by The Historical Games Company as a replica of the original game, English, 1994.

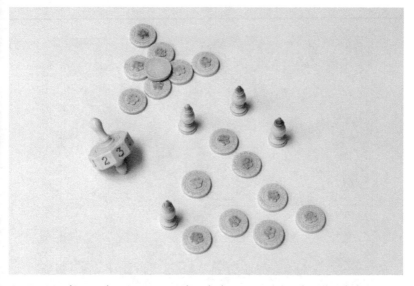

54. Die, markers and counters. Issued with the new game and made of plastic representing bone.

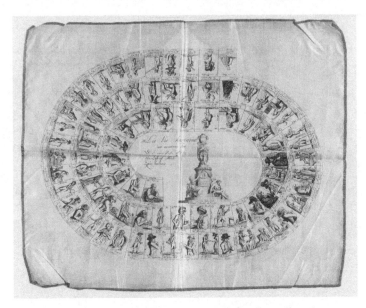

Above: 55. *La Vie Humaine, Un Nouveau Jeu.* Printed on silk and published by Simon Schropp; German, about 1800.

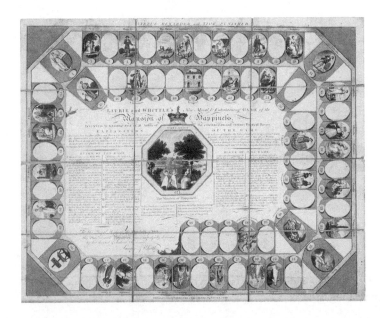

57. *Every Man to His Station*. Published by The Historical Games Company as a replica of the original game, English, 1994.

Right: 58. *Snakes and Ladders.*

Opposite below: 56. Laurie and Whittle's *New Moral and Entertaining Game of The Mansion of Happiness*[4] subtitled *Virtue Rewarded and Vice Punished.* Published by Robert Laurie and James Whittle, 53 Fleet Street, London, 13 October 1800.

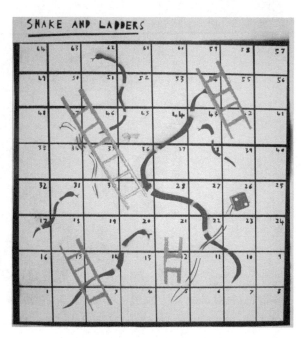

59. *Pachisi*. Various woods and cowrie shells, made by James Masters, English, 2006.

60. *Ludo*. Wood, stained and painted, made by James Masters, English, 2006.

61. *Monopoly.*[5] Manufactured and distributed by Waddington Games Ltd, England.

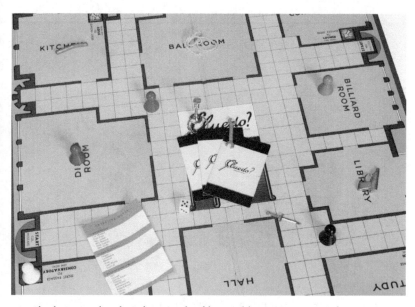

62. *Cluedo.* Printed and made in England by Waddington Games Ltd.

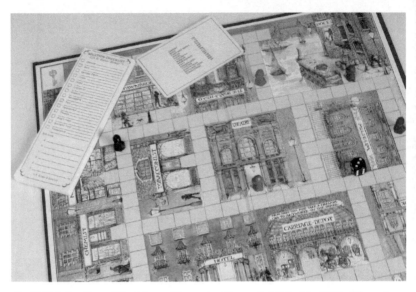

63. *221B Baker Street*, The Master Detective Game. Published by H.P. Gibson & Sons Ltd.

64. *The Grosvenor Series*. Published *c.* 1920 by Charles & Son.

65. *Boggle*. Tonka Corporation © 1992.

66. *Pictionary*. Published by Parker Games © 1987.

67. *Totally Dingbats*. Published by Waddingtons Games Ltd, 1990/1992. Game devised by Paul Sellers. Dingbats® is a registered trade mark of Paul Sellers, for the game manufactured and sold under exclusive licence to Waddingtons Games Ltd.

68. *My Word*. Published by W.H. Storey & Co. Ltd. of Croydon, *c.* 1930.

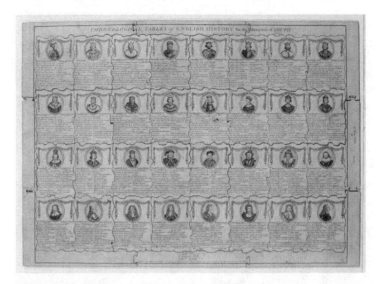

69. *The Kings of England, William I to Queen Victoria*. Dissected puzzle, hand-coloured engraving mounted on wood and cut into twenty-nine non-interlocking pieces. This puzzle was probably the work of Nicholas Carpenter, Goswell Terrace, London who produced a similar puzzle about 1832 using his own imprint in the space occupied by Queen Victoria.

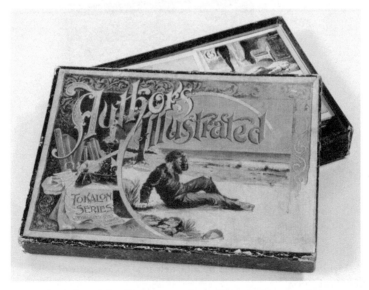

70. *Authors Illustrated*. Tokalon Series © 1893 by Clark & Sowdon, USA.

71. *Game of Authors*. Published by Milton Bradley, USA, 1910.

72. *Vignette Authors*. Published by E.G. Selchow & Company of New York, 1874.

Snakes and Ladders

By the mid-nineteenth century, moral games were very much on the decline. Nevertheless, an Indian game by the name of *Moksha-Patamu* actually taught the rudiments of rewards for good behaviour and punishment for bad. It was an ancient game with ladders representing good and elevating the players towards heaven and snakes representing bad and going down to the abyss. The religious teachings had four virtues (faith, reliability, generosity and knowledge) but twelve vices (disobedience, vanity, vulgarity, theft, lying, drinking, debt, anger, avarice, pride, killing and lust).

The attributes of the game appealed to the later Victorian parents as a suitable way to teach good behaviour. They were not worried about the influence of dice so these became the tools governing the movement of the markers on the board. In 1892, F.H. Ayers patented spiral snakes and ladders with five of each. Before the end of the century, a number of different games based on the same principles were devised. *Kismet*, published about 1895 as part of the Globe Series, had only eight ladders against thirteen snakes. There were obvious illustrations, such as Pride leading down a snake to a picture of a man falling but the good elements lead only to Virtue.

Another *Snakes and Ladders* board published about the same time, shows both pictures and sayings to illustrate the theme. One of the more surprising is Punctuality leading up to Opulence. The board also has names of famous people on a scroll at the end, square 100. These names are also in other squares, for example Perseverance leads up to 'Watt, Livingstone, Washington, etc.'

As the twentieth century progressed, the moral overtones of *Snakes and Ladders* were removed and replaced with a simple game of winning or losing that even the youngest player could attempt. It even became a game based on a film character, that of Charlie Chaplin's 'Little Tramp'. Most of this game reflected the character's uphill battle for achievement.

The other great modern game with much history is *Ludo*. Classified now as a simple game it is another governed by the throw of a die. Along with *Snakes and Ladders*, *Ludo* is often the first game a young child learns to play as the rules are simple and no reading is required. It is also a fast game so a child's interest in it has no chance to wane.

The game is taken from the Indian game called *Pachisi*, and it was brought to England in the late nineteenth century. One of the early *Ludo* games was registered by John Jaques & Son Ltd as *The Popular Game of Patchesi* in 1887 using an X-shaped design rather than the cross shape used in India. It is, however, a game that appeared elsewhere in North and South America before European colonisation. It is also played in Africa where, like *Mancala*, it is a very rapid game.

The traditional Indian game is now played on a cloth that resembles patchwork. It could be made by scratching the design on the ground and has been found on stone carvings. The four arms have three rows each and the centre where the arms meet is the 'home'. The game may be played with long wooden dice, each side marked with combinations of circles or with six cowrie shells as dice. If these are used the number is counted from the shells landing with their openings up. If no openings show, the player is allocated twenty-five and an extra throw.

The normal game is played by up to four people and each has four markers. The aim is to get all of one's markers into the home or centre first. Each player starts on one arm and moves one marker forward depending on the throw of the dice. A new marker may only be introduced on the throw of six. The markers move around the outside rows of each of the arms until they reach their own starting arm at which time they proceed up the centre row to the 'home'. Modern *Ludo* games tend to be colour-coordinated so green starts on green, for example.

On each arm, there are three safe squares but on any other square markers can be taken by an opponent if his marker lands on the same square. The captured markers are removed and must start again.

Between 1900 and 1940, a number of the major games publishers produced their own versions of *Ludo*. There were some adaptations too. In the 1950s, John Waddington Ltd patented *Skudo*. The board is similarly marked to a Ludo game with the cross and squares layout, but four movable circles are added in the corners. If a marker lands on the *Skudo* square, the player is allowed to turn the circle so that the marker may pass, and this shortens the player's route around the board. These are the rules Waddington's gave their game:

The game can be played by 2, 3 or 4 players, each player choosing one of the four colours. Before play commences, each of the DISCS must be set so the 'Red can Pass', faces 'Red Starts' in the Red corner, 'Green can pass' faces 'Green Starts' in the Green Corner and so on. Counters are placed in the spaces at each side of the 'Start' spaces, 4 to each player. The first player throws the dice and moves one counter the number of spaces scores (counting Start as 1) towards the centre of the disc, and then to the left which is the nearest way to get around the board to reach HOME the objective. Each player follows in turn.

When a 6 is scored, a player is entitled, if he so desires, to revolve any one disc to bring the sector colour to allow the passage of his own colour counter or prevent opponents from moving their counters across, also the player moves a counter 6 spaces and takes an additional throw.

A counter reaching a space marked SKUDO entitles the player to revolve the nearest disc only. In all cases, discs must always be turned so that pathways join, but they can be turned a quarter, half or three quarters round.

Discs must face the correct way before counters can move across – Red can Pass for red counters, etc. Scores being forfeited until a 6 or SKUDO is scored, enabling the disc to be revolved to allow passage.

A player revolving a disc may cause a counter already on the disc to be moved to the top above the centre and this counter can then only proceed by being moved around the curved path thereby being handicapped by the additional spaces to be scored, or by a player scoring a 6 or a SKUDO enabling the disc to be moved again.

Any number of player's 4 counters can be brought into play at will.

Whenever a counter moves on to a space occupied by an opponent, the opponent's counter returns to the starting point. If 2 counters or more are covered all are moved back.

Counters must move completely round the board before entering 'HOME' and the correct number required to reach Home must be scored, higher score being ignored.

The player to get all counters Home first is the winner. If it is desired to play shorter game, players can each use 2 or 3 counters only.

John Waddington Ltd was also responsible for a second variation on *Ludo*, which had the name *Sorry*, later to be renamed *The Great Game of Sorry*. The company applied for its patent in 1929 and in the 1934 catalogue of the American firm Parker Brothers it was listed as 'the most fashionable and largest selling game in England'. John Waddington Ltd and Parker Brothers collaborated on quite a number of games, both board and card games. John Waddington Ltd was primarily a card publishing company and this new game combined cards and a playing surface. The game was played exactly the same way as *Ludo*, but instead of dice, cards were used to determine the play.

Salida, the Spanish word for 'exit', is a rather interesting game that looks like *Ludo* and is played in the same manner. Markers would be used with each player starting on one or at a starting point on the arm matching their colour. On each of the arms are two black circles and one matching colour strip leading off to the right to join a hole cut into the board. Each hole contains a dice and is covered by a clear plastic cap. On the edge of the board by each hole is a triangular plastic trigger that operates a mechanism below the dice to toss it. The number of moves would be determined by the toss of the dice. If a player lands on the square marked 'SALIDA' leading to the dice, he would have the opportunity to toss the number to exit via the coloured triangle. If the correct number was not tossed, he would continue around the board. The board is numbered 1 to 102.

In 1983, Galt Toys published two *Ludo* games, one bearing trees and fruit is played by the same rules and is of a decorative design that would appeal to young children. The second game, aimed at slightly older children, is *Tracks*. In this game there are still only up to four players but as they move around the game cards of tracks or footprints must be matched. The tracks are those of a sled, paw print, boots, hooves and birds. There is a spinner of white plastic; it shows six compartments, which correspond to the item that made the tracks together with a snowman that does not make a track. The rules are simple.

Place all the cards face down on the table. Each player chooses ten cards which may then be arranged face up beside the board. The remaining face down cards form a 'pool'.

In turn each player spins the disc and depending on which figure stops at the end of his or her path lays a matching track card.

The snowman leaves no tracks and a player may use the plain white side of any card if the snowman stops at the end of a path.

If the player does not have a matching track card, he may exchange one of his cards with a card from the pool. Only one card per turn may be exchanged in this way. If the disc stops exactly between two figures the turn is taken again.

The winner is the first player to complete a path.

Like many other games now, *Snakes and Ladders* and *Ludo* have been adapted and redesigned many times and are now available as computer games and as large-scale games used in schools, parks and hotels.

Monopoly and Cluedo

The twentieth century produced three great games that have been adapted, copied and are now available online. These three are *Monopoly*, *Cluedo* and *Scrabble* (see Spelling chapter). Of these, *Monopoly* is the most reproduced of all manufactured games.

Monopoly, according to the manufacturers, is said to have been invented by Charles Darrow and presented to Parker Brothers, the American games publishers, in 1934. By 1936, it was being produced in England by John Waddington Ltd. However, the history of the game goes much further back to 1904 and an American lady called Elizabeth M. Phillips who, with friends, produced a similar game to illustrate commercial dealings and the buying and selling of land. Called the *Landlord's Game*, it became a teaching aid and the Religious Society of Friends sold their handmade copies. It may be that Charles Darrow used one of these games but failed to reveal its source. In England before the First World War, *Brer Fox and Brer Rabbit*, reflecting the political aspect of the game, was published with almost the same rules as the later *Monopoly* game. During the 1920s and 1930s, several similar games were published by different manufacturers including *Big Business* by the Transgram Company. This particular game combined the financial strengths and weaknesses of each of the American states. Parker Brothers also manufactured *Bulls and Bears*, a game about the stock market. Nevertheless, it is *Monopoly* that has survived and grown through adaptation.

The original game consisted of a playing surface, property cards and direction cards together with play money. The markers were made of lead and the dice wood or celluloid. With resumption of manufacture after the Second World War, many materials were in short supply for a number of years revealing the desperate plight of the British Toy Industry when materials were not available for trivial use. Games of this period reflect this with printed card markers and a card spinner replacing the dice. Many toys and games produced between 1945 and 1952 showed the austerity in their production but many of them were destroyed when new ones were available.

The original version of what is now *Monopoly* was based on streets and areas in the American town Atlantic City. It consisted of forty squares, of which twenty-eight were properties, a Jail and Go to Jail, Free Parking, three Chance and Community Chest squares each, two Tax squares and the Go or start square. The adaptations are many, especially those designed for other countries. At first a town or city in a particular country would be designated and the properties assigned names from it. Later editions and special editions have been made reflecting many different towns or cities in many countries.

Likewise, the play money used in the game has been adapted for the country as have some of the terms. For example, in British versions, the pound replaces the dollar and tax becomes a flat rate tax and a super tax. John Waddington Ltd obtained a licence for both the production and marketing of the game outside the United States. The company replaced the property names with suitable London ones, each one with a history of its own:

    The Strand
    Fleet Street
    Trafalgar Square
    Leicester Square
    Coventry Street
    Piccadilly
    Vine Street
    Regent Street
    Marlborough Street
    Oxford Street
    Bow Street
    Bond Street
    Northumberland Avenue
    Whitehall
    Park Lane
    Pall Mall
    Mayfair
    Pentonville Road
    Euston Road
    The Angel, Islington
    Whitechapel Road
    Old Kent Road

To these streets were added Fenchurch Street Station, Marylebone Station, Liverpool Street Station and Kings' Cross Station. The Go, Free Parking, Go to Jail and Jail squares remained the same as did the tax, utilities, community chest and chance squares. As the game has been adapted, it has also been modernised with different playing pieces reflecting new ideas such as mobile phones, laptops and a jumbo jet. In 2007 Hasbro, now the manufacturer, introduced other British cities as part of the 'Here and Now Editions'.

The aim of the game is to make money by buying and selling properties as well as renting them. The various named properties are banded with colours, usually three to a group, sometimes only two. As the game proceeds, it is to the player's advantage to own all the properties in one colour band. Each player is allotted an equal sum of money from which to buy a property or pay a bill. The rest of the money is kept in the 'bank' and one of the players is elected banker.

The game is supplied with six markers,[1] two dice, a quantity of green houses and red hotels, cards representing the title deeds for the properties, community chest and chance cards and play money in the denominations £500, £100, £50, £20, £10, £5 and £1.[2] The community chest and chance cards are placed on the board face down, in designated places. The players, having selected their marker, throw the dice and commence the game. The first player moves from the Go square the number of squares shown on the dice. Depending on where he lands he has the chance of buying the property, paying taxes, going to jail or taking one of the community chest or chance cards. If a double is thrown, he may throw again. Each time a player completes a circuit of the board and passes Go he receives £200 as a salary from the bank, unless he has been directed to go to jail.

If the player can afford to buy the property he lands on, the bank is paid the set sum and the player receives the appropriate card. As the game proceeds, most of the properties will be bought and if a player has a complete colour band set, he may erect a house on his 'land' and with enough houses, a hotel. Such an owner may also double the rent paid by anyone landing on his property. The rates for houses, hotels and rents are listed on the property cards.

Should the player land on either of the community chest or chance squares, he must take the appropriate card from the pile and do whatever directed to do. Sometimes it is a reward such as money, other times it is a forfeit such as paying money out. If the player is sent to jail, there are three ways he may get out of it again. He will have the chance to throw a double on his next three turns. Alternatively, he may have or purchase from any player a 'Get out of Jail' card. On the other hand, he pays the fine of £50. However, if after three turns he is still in jail, he must pay the fine. Then again, while in jail he may still collect rents on his properties.

Not all players will continue to gain money, some will have to mortgage their property, again the rates are on the title deeds, or they may declare themselves bankrupt. At this point, he must leave the game.

Monopoly may take many hours to play and often result in no overall winner. The winner is decided by totalling all the properties, money, houses and hotels each player owns and the one with the greatest amount wins. There are several ways to shorten the game with the easiest having a time limit. Having reached the limit, the counting begins as before. Another way is to deal a set number of cards to each player, usually two, at the beginning of the game.

As with many other games, *Monopoly* tournaments are held. The game can also be played online.

Cluedo, or *Clue*, is a game with international connections. Originally devised in England by Anthony Pratt of Birmingham, it made its appearance in 1948 published by John Waddington Ltd. The present-day versions are published by Hasbro as part of the Parker Games series. As a crime fiction game, it has some mystery of its own. It is thought that the game may be based on Scalford Hall, Leicestershire, once owned by a Colonel Colman of Colman's Mustard.[3] Certainly, the game is based on rooms in a mansion, owned by the victim, Mr Black, and the board is divided into the hall, lounge, dining room, kitchen, ballroom, conservatory, billiard room, library, and study. It is complimented with its own secret passageways. The aim for the players acting as detectives is to discover who was murderer, where and with what instrument. There are six characters that are used by the players: Colonel Mustard, Prof. Plum, The Rev. Green, Mrs Peacock, Miss Scarlett and Mrs White.[4] There are six murder weapons: dagger, candlestick, revolver, rope, lead pipe and a spanner. Each element of the game has its own card, six each for the characters and weapons, nine for the house.

Before the game commences, each pack of cards is shuffled and one card chosen at random. The three cards are then placed into a provided envelope, which is only to be opened at the end of the game. The rest of the cards are shuffled together and dealt to each of the players who may now look at the cards without revealing them to the others. Unlike most games, the players have specific starting points. None is more advantaged than another is, but Miss Scarlett always moves first. On the throw of the dice, the marker may be moved along the passage to any room chosen. Play continues until one player reaches a room at which time he may make a 'suggestion'. He suggests one character with one instrument in one room. If the next player has one of the cards mentioned, it must be shown to the first player. If this player has no cards, the duty goes to the next and so on until one card is shown. If no one is holding a particular card, it may be assumed that the card is in the envelope. Play continues until one player is certain he has worked out who was the murderer, what weapon he used and where the crime was committed. He may then make an 'accusation'; if correct, he is the winner. If, however, he is wrong he retires from the game except to assist others when they make a 'suggestion' if he holds a particular card.

It is quite permissible to give 'bluff suggestions', by suggesting as one clue a card he holds himself. This may give the details of the whereabouts of a particular card while misleading the other players. The rules for play are quite harsh, for example if a player fails to show a card that would indicate that it was out of play, he must stop playing and may only join in at the suggestion time to show cards. The markers must enter the rooms via the doorways and must not block the entrance except from outside the rooms. Once in a room the player's turn finishes. If the secret passageways are used, it is a move and the dice may not be thrown as well.

A certain amount of strategy is required to be successful and two players may enjoy the game, however, with the introduction of more players, the odds are changed and the degree of complexity increased. For players it is wise not to keep making the same suggestion each time, merely changing one element. The other players will soon find out who is suspected of doing the dastardly deed with what and where.

Cluedo has had many adaptations including films and television as well as the computer and video versions. As the game has become international, there are slight variations. The adaptations sometimes have the victim Mr Black and a detective, which the board game does not. In the board game Mr Black is only listed as the victim and does not make an appearance. The players are the detectives.

There are few detective games that could rival *Cluedo*, however, *221B Baker Street, The Master Detective Game* does. As the name suggests it is based on the cases of the fictional Sherlock Holmes. In the stories, written by Arthur Conan Doyle, the great detective lived at the London address given. The playing board is illustrated with fourteen locations starting with 221B Baker Street, Chemist shop, Newsagent, Locksmith, Pawnbroker, The Boar's Head pub, Docks, Museum, Bank, Scotland Yard and Park around the outer edges with Hotel, Tobacconist, Theatre and Carriage Depot[5] in the centre. The rules quote Sherlock Holmes: 'It is of the highest importance in the art of detection to be able to recognise, out of a number of facts, which are incidental and which are vital.'

With the game are six markers, in coloured plastic moulded to show the head of Sherlock Holmes, six Scotland Yard[6] and skeleton keys cards,[7] forty case cards, booklet of clues, rules and solutions and a die. Additionally a scratch pad has been provided to mark down ideas and solutions. All the players start in Baker Street, and on the throw of the die move off in any direction to any of the other sites. Clues are provided at each place.[8] These are noted on the reverse of the case cards with an assigned key number given in the booklet. Each player is also allocated one Scotland Yard card to seal off any location from other players entering it, and one skeleton key to open any sealed-off site. Although a player may not have more than one of each of these cards, he may collect a new one if he visits Scotland Yard or the Locksmiths.

Interestingly, in the Elementary Rules given in the booklet, it is suggested that one player reads the Case out loud to the others. This is not done in modern games very often but was prevalent in eighteenth- and nineteenth-century games. The aim of the game is to solve the case, return to 221B Baker Street and announce the solution. By studying one case, it is easier to follow the rules.

Case No. 5, The Adventure of the Kidnapped Infant
The two-month old daughter of the Duke and Duchess of Crescentshire has been kidnapped. Nanny Ann Whiston, who was taking the baby for a walk in the Park, says that a man accosted her, grabbed the baby from its carriage and disappeared in the direction of the Chemist.

After five days, the Duke and Duchess have still not heard from the kidnapper. The Duke, who wanted a son and was quite disappointed when he learned that his first born was a girl, has done nothing more about the kidnapping than to draw it to the attention of Scotland Yard.

Based on the description provided by Nanny Whiston, Scotland Yard has identified three chief suspects from its file known kidnap specialists. The suspects are Anton Aldred, Jeremy Bridges, and Bill 'Stonewall' Jackson. Aldred and Bridges kidnap strictly for ransom money, whilst Jackson specialises in selling babies on the black market.

Completely distraught over the strange disappearance of her daughter, The Duchess of Crescentshire has come to 221B Baker Street for help. The Duchess wants Holmes to discover a) who kidnapped her daughter, b) the whereabouts of the infant, and c) the motive.

The game is afoot!

Within the story are the locations, the people and what the player is expected to discover. Should the player first visit the Park, he will then have the opportunity of looking at the clue for that location which states: 'Ann Whiston has worked as a governess and nanny for nearly twenty years'. This is a straightforward statement clue, however, some clues refer to the motive, killer or weapon and these are always four-part clues, none of which individually solve the problem.

When a player thinks he has all the clues and knows the answers to the questions posed, he must return to Baker Street. He then becomes Sherlock Holmes and the rest of the players Dr Watson. The correct solution to this case is: 'after twenty years of caring for other people's children, Ann Whiston yearned for a child of her own. Knowing that the Duke of Crescentshire did not appreciate his daughter anyway, Governess Whiston decided to steal the baby and raise it herself. She hid the infant in her husband's fishing boat.' From the clue cited a player would have no reason to suspect the governess, especially as the police had three good suspects.

The game *221B Baker Street* was copyrighted by Jay Moriarty in 1975 and manufactured by H.P. Gibson & Sons Ltd. It is an intriguing game requiring more abilities than *Cluedo*. It also takes longer to play each game, however, if the players enjoy both good mysteries and the Sherlock Holmes adventures this is the game to play.

Spelling

Spelling made easy might have been the intention of many games, but the child rarely viewed it that way. Spelling, like grammar, is a discipline to be exercised whereas reading is enjoyable.

Many games required the child to read out the answers from provided text. Spelling tended to be taught with letters of the alphabet. Early games simply provided twenty-six counters, sometimes of wood or cardboard, sometimes of bone. The counters may be marked with the upper-case letter on one side and the lower-case letter on the reverse or they might have an illustration of a suitable object. As the nineteenth century progressed, sets became larger as additional letters were added so more words could be formed.

Word and picture matching was another way of attempting to teach spelling. By matching a series of drawings to their appropriate name the child was expected to learn the letters. Nevertheless, one wonders how a child who did not know how to spell could decide which group of letters was right. Some degree of knowledge of the alphabet and the pronunciation of the letters had to be learned before the game was undertaken.

Boggle, The 3 Minute Word Game, uses sixteen cubes with letters on all sides. The aim is to list as many words as possible from a random selection of letters. The cubes are shaken and a time limit imposed. This game was copyrighted by the Tonka Corporation in 1992 and is a sophisticated version of a game called *Shake Spell* that had five lettered cubes. The more cubes there are makes an easier game and younger children whose vocabulary is limited have more of a chance of winning.

Pictionary is a game that relies on a drawing to depict a word. Copyrighted in 1987 and made by Parker Games, now part of Hasbro, the game combines several activities that are inter-dependent on each other. There is the playing surface round which the players' markers move, a die to be thrown which governs the moves, a timing device and the all-important question cards. In the game there are 500 cards divided into five categories – people, places and animals; objects that can be seen or touched; action or things that can be done; challenging words and any type of word. The players work as teams and one team member is then chosen to draw the pictures; this is rotated after each picture is solved.

Play begins when one player selects a card, studies it briefly then must draw a picture, within a given time period, that will illustrate what word was on the card. No letters may be used or any other form of assistance from the artist. Once the word is identified within the time limit, the die is thrown and the marker moved forward. If the word is not found, play moves to the next team who select a fresh card and the process continues. The die is only thrown when a picture has been successfully identified. These rules apply to the first four categories but the fifth, All Play, is a free-for-all attempt at guessing the word. All the people selected to do the drawing at that time are shown the card. Whichever team finds the solution within the time limit throws the die and moves accordingly. Any number may occupy the same square and a team must stay on a square until it identifies a new word.

To win, a team must reach the last All Play square and be the first to identify the chosen word. If the team fails to do so, the game continues until the team regains the control of the die and attempt to identify a word again. Although the exact roll of the die affects the rest of the teams, it does not apply to this team. If the team correctly identifies the word, it is declared the winner.

There are two further suggestions given in the rules about the players and the answers. First, the publishers suggest that play is quicker and more exciting if there are less teams and more players per team. However, should there only be three players, one acts as the person who selects the cards and draws the pictures throughout the game. The normal rules apply to the other two players.

Secondly the publishers suggest that the teams must decide before the start of the game how precise the answers must be, for example is 'Bunk' acceptable for 'Bunk bed'?

As with many games, *Pictionary* has international tournaments and like so many modern games is available for play on the computer and over the last thirty years has been the inspiration for a number of television game shows.

Picture and word recognition is the theme behind the game of *Totally Dingbats*. Devised by Paul Sellers and copyrighted in 1990, the game was first made by Waddingtons Games Ltd. It is a game to solve rebuses, or puzzles with hidden words or sayings within an arrangement of symbols or a cryptic. The game has a playing board, 576 cards divided into Dingbats, Kingbats and Thinkbats, one ordinary die and one specially marked die, and six markers[1] to be moved around the board. Again, there is a time limit imposed. The aim of the game is to solve each of the *Dingbats* and reach the winner's enclosure where a final solving of a KINGBAT will decide the winner. Each of the cards has the rebus on one side and the solution on the other.

On the throw of the dice, the player's marker is moved and he will be required to solve the puzzle depending on what square is landed on.[2] The person next to him selects the appropriate card, without looking at the answer. The specially marked die will indicate whether the player alone must answer the rebus, or one or all of the other players may compete against him. The person who selected the card does not play in this round. Play continues until one player reaches the winner's enclosure.

There are a number of rules determining whether a guess is challenged, whether two people have called out the same answer at the same time or whether guesses are right or wrong. The Moderator, who is not actively part of the round, is the decision maker and the moves of the markers are based on his decision. There are shortcuts on the board, allowing players to advance quickly but there are penalties for wrong answers and challenges where players' markers are moved backwards on the board.

The winning square on the board does not have to be reached by a definite number and a marker will remain there until the game is won, or the marker switched with another player's one. On reaching the winning square, the player must solve a Kingbat card to win.

This is a challenging game for young children but a good family game for all ages to enjoy. It too has an online version.

The ultimate spelling game is *Scrabble*. This game requires the key elements of vocabulary, arithmetic and strategy as well as spelling. Designed for two, three or four players it was a game devised in the 1930s by an American, Alfred Butts. At that stage there was no board, merely lettered tiles to be arranged as words. By the end of the 1930s, the board had been added and the game became a crossword puzzle. J.W. Spear & Sons Ltd produced the game for the English and Australian markets from the 1950s. The game has hardly changed in all its years. The first tiles were made of wood and these are now of plastic. Occasionally a new edition or special edition is introduced and in 1983, J.W. Spear & Sons Ltd marketed *Scrabble for Juniors*. This board combined pictorial images along with letters and a young child could play it even if they were unable to spell. The images were linked to the letters so a player needed only to find the letter that matched that on the board.

The game is still very popular and international and national tournaments are held. The board has 225 squares, arranged in a pattern of 15 x 15, and a number are marked for extra points. Each of the ninety-eight tiles is numbered and these are added up at the end of the placing of a word. An additional two blank tiles may be used for any letter. Each player selects seven tiles from which he must make a word or forego his turn. Once the first word is down the rest may be linked to it, in other words a new word may be created from some or all of the letters of the first word, so long as the resulting word is in the dictionary. No nouns or offensive words are permitted. When a player uses tiles, he must draw more to keep his number at seven. This is repeated until there are no tiles left. The aim is to have the highest score.

The *Scrabble* tiles are generally kept in a cloth bag and drawn out as necessary. Other games also use this method of acquiring some of their playing pieces, notably the games of *Lotto*. Not to be confused with the lottery games, *Lotto* is an alternative name for *Bingo*. *Lotto* has always primarily been a game of chance. In the case for *Lotto* for children to play, publishers decided to use the same format to make an educational game that was fun as well.

John Jaques & Son Ltd published a number of these games, but they were not alone and many publishers produced games of varying difficulty. History and foreign languages were popular subjects, but one of the more unusual was *Floral Lotto*, published by Jaques in the 1870s. The game has twelve boards, each with ten images in colours of different flowers. With the game are 120 oval discs printed with the common name, the botanical name and the emblematical significance of each flower.

To play the game the players must randomly select a small card, usually from a bag, and correctly identify the picture on the large board and cover it. The player of course may not have the picture relating to the card selected, in which case the card is returned to the bag to be drawn again at random.

Many publishers produced *Lotto* or *Bingo* for children to play. It was popular in compendiums of games, which would include a number of board and card games. Throughout the twentieth century, *Lotto* using animal or other household items was published. There was always an attempt to steer away from the gambling element of the game.

Lotto could become a question and answer game and an early version was *Answerit?* published by The Chad Valley Company in the mid-1920s. Its descendent is *Trivial Pursuits*. This is a game now adapted many times for different subjects. The normal general knowledge questions can be replaced with specific subjects like sports, books and the cinema.

Card Games

Playing cards were introduced into Europe from China in the late fourteenth century. At the time, they were not for children to play with although, should they have come across a pack, it is probable that a game would have been the result. Cards specifically designed for children were introduced in the mid-eighteenth century by the same publishers who developed the board games. It was because these publishers had the necessary printing equipment coupled with the ideas and illustrations already directed at children.

The first games were not played as such; the cards were instruments of learning. The majority were educational, teaching geography, science, natural science, arithmetic and languages. As more of the world was explored, so all the finds, including flora and fauna, were added. Often the sets were accompanied by booklets, which described the cards in the same manner as the games.

One of the earliest card games is *Pastora, or the Shepherdess of the Pyrenees. A Diverting Game; calculated to kill care and enliven the dreary hours of winter.* It is really a board game cum whist game played with a deck of cards, but these are important to the game.

Published in 1796 by Champante & Whitrow, with a booklet printed for E. Newbery, Corner of St Paul's Churchyard, by J. Cundee, Ivy Lane, the playing sheet shows in the corners representations of playing cards – King of Hearts, Queen of Spades, Jack of Clubs, 10 of Diamonds. At this time, it was rare for children to play with real cards for the same reasons as dice, but this was a family game for everyone to enjoy.

John Wallis published in 1799 a true child's game based on geography. It had the grand title *The Geography of England and Wales accurately delineated* with a footnote to the rules that states, '… by which means the cards will render not only instructive but amusing and entertaining.' With the game are fifty-two cards, each giving a county of England or Wales, describing the boundaries, principal towns, products and general characteristics together with a letterpress sheet of directions for play and a general description of England and Wales. This set was published at the beginning of the Industrial Revolution and it shows the move away from agriculture to industry.

At this time, most games required forfeiture. The usual family game had all the cards dealt out with one player elected as leader to ask the questions. In the case of geography, he might ask what river a town is beside, and the players answer referring to their lowest card number. If correct, the card is withdrawn and the player rewarded with a counter from the kitty. If wrong, the player must keep his card and pay a counter into the kitty. The winner is the one who gets rid of his cards; he then becomes the leader.

Language games, either to learn English or a foreign tongue, tended to be in the form of question and answer. For English lessons, it would be a pack of questions usually related to grammar, such as explain the tenses, with a second pack providing the answers. Sometimes the element of gambling was introduced to make the game more exciting. Rewards were paid to the player for a right answer and forfeits paid by the player for a wrong one. Such a game was published about

1790 entitled *Grammatical Conversations or English Grammar Familiarised*. This type of game would require an older child or an adult to control the play.

Foreign languages, also taught on cards, may have three or four translations. Italian, Spanish and Polish may be added to English, French and German. The normal game would cite good and bad behaviour and moral teachings, again reflecting the attitude to these principles. One game of this type, *Le Petit Questionneur Polyglotte*, states it is a proper exercise to excite children about conversation. One feels that the normal child would find other games more exciting.

By the middle of the nineteenth century, new types of card games were being developed for children, as learning tools and for amusement. The foremost English publisher at this time was John Jaques & Son of London. The company developed three games, two of which are still played – *Happy Families*, *Snap* and *The Counties of England*. The latter of which is no longer played, but at the time of its introduction in 1866, it was an enjoyable way to learn about the counties. Three sets were eventually produced, usually of sixty-one cards divided into thirteen counties and the rest principal towns. There was not a set number for each county; some had five or six cards to complete it, others only three. The aim was to complete a county by collecting the town cards to match it. There were two simple sets of rules and again with the second set of rules, a gambling element is introduced.

Any number above three can play. The cards to be shuffled and dealt round. The player next to the dealer (or the winner of a previous round) begins the game by asking for a card of any county of which he holds either a town or the county card. If he gets it, he continues asking for what he wants till he is refused. Then the privilege of asking devolves upon the player who refused him; he in his turn asks for any card he requires to complete his set, until he is refused, and so the game goes on.

When a player has the County card in his hand he knows how many towns he requires to make up a set. Every set made up is proclaimed and laid down on the table.

The player who has made up most sets is winner when the cards are all played out, and has the privilege of the first question at the next round.

Any player withholding a card asked for, forfeits a set. Disputes to be settled by reference to the key.

OR THE GAME MAY BE PLAYED THUS:-

1. One player to be chosen as President.

2. The president to retain the county cards, and deal the picture cards round.

3. Six counters to be given to each player and some put in the pool.

4. The president to ask each player in turn for a card of the town belonging to the country which he mentions.

5. If a card of another county is offered, the person forfeits one to the pool; but if the right one is offered, he takes one from the pool.

6. Any person relating a fact or describing scenery, manufactures, etc. connected with his card, receives an additional counter from the pool.

7. The sets being all made up, he who has the most counters wins.

Having developed this game, Jaques & Son Ltd went on to issue such games as *The New Game of Illustrated Proverbs* and *A Game of Hide and Seek with the Kings and Queens of England*, played by the same rules.

Happy Families, also introduced by Jaques, has remained one of the all-time favourites for children to play. This game, along with *Snap*, was truly a game for entertainment rather than learning. The original design was by Sir John Tenniel, the illustrator of Lewis Carroll's *Alice's Adventures in Wonderland*

and *Through the Looking Glass*. The game was simple with sets of four cards making a 'family' – father, mother, girl and boy. The families represented occupations and the names given reflected the jobs, for example Mr Bun the Baker.

The rules are simple but competitive. All the cards are dealt, and the player to the left of the dealer starts by asking any of the other players for a character he or she is short of to complete a set. The player should endeavour to collect all the cards relating to one family and when the four cards are held, they are placed, face downwards, as a trick, on the table. The word trick is really a misnomer in this game, as the aim is to collect a sequence and not to trump other cards.

If a player asked has not got the character, he or she replies 'Not at home' and it becomes his or her turn to ask.

The game proceeds until all the family sets are complete, and the player holding the greatest number of tricks wins. Players cannot ask for characters unless they already hold a member of the family, and players are bound to produce the character asked for if they have it.

The game can end here or continue following other rules. Only players holding tricks continue, and the one with the greatest number starts. He or she asks any other player for a family. If the player asked does not have the family, it then becomes his or her turn. The game ends when one player holds all the families.

An element of gambling can be introduced if each player puts up an agreed number of counters into a pool. The winner of the first part of the game takes half the kitty, and the winner of the second part takes the rest.

An interesting extra to the rules of play incorporated into some of these card games is the paying of a special forfeit. Instead of just losing a turn, a player must allow an unseen card to be drawn from his hand by an opponent.

General Happy Families Rules

Three or more can play and special cards are normally used, each showing four members of a family: mother, father, son and daughter. However, variations have been developed to use groups of 3, 4, 5, 6, and 7 to a set. Also subject variations occur and some are educational, for example *The Counties of England*.

The object of the game is for each player to collect as many complete 'families' as possible.

One of the players deals out all the cards. If more than one round is played, the players take it in turn to deal. It does not matter if some players have one card more than others.

Each player looks at his cards and sorts them into families.

It is important that players keep their cards hidden from each other. With young children it is a good idea if they can lay their cards out of view of the other players.

When all the players are ready, the person to the dealer's left asks any player, by name, for a particular card (e.g. Master Baker). He must already possess at least one of member of the same family, i.e. Mrs Baker. If the person asked has the card, he must give it to the first player, who may again ask anybody for a card of any family as long as he already has one card belonging to that family.

He continues to do this until he fails to obtain a card. If the person asked does not have the card requested, it is his turn to ask for cards.

When a player collects all the cards of the same family, he puts them into a pile face down in front of him.

Play continues until all the families have been completed

The winner is the person who collects the most families.

Before 1900, many other publishers were producing their own versions of *Happy Families* using other names to avoid legal actions. For example Mrs Alliston of London printed *Merry Families* containing all animals such as cats and goats; *Funny Families* was produced by J.W. Spear & Sons using caricatures. In the United States, W. & S.B. Ives printed the *Game of Trades*, which may actually be the forerunner of Jaques' card game. It had some picture cards and others with matching symbols, which had to be collected to make a set, more like *The Counties of England* to play.

In 1897, the American company the US Playing Card Co. of Cincinnati published a range of children's card games with an educational theme. These were sold in Great Britain by a leading publisher of children's puzzles and games, H.P. Gibson & Sons Ltd. The games included *Authors*, *Famous Paintings*, *In Castle Land*, *Flowers* and *Artists*.

The rules for the games include several sets that could be played depending on the age and abilities of the players. For example in the *Authors*, the pack represents the works of leading world writers. There are four sets of thirteen cards numbered thirteen to one and lettered A, B, C and D. These rules show how diverse the games could be and the games are recognisable by different names.

RULES FOR PLAYING THE GAME OF AUTHORS, NO. 1119, COPYRIGHT 1897 BY THE US PLAYING CARD CO, CINCINNATI USA

The rules of the well-known game of *Authors* apply. A book consists of the cards of the four authors whose names are printed in heavy type thereon, and having the same index number; thus, the four 1's.

Deal four cards to each player and lay the pack on the table face down. Each player, beginning at the dealer's left calls from any of the other players the name of the author, for a card to complete or help complete a book, part of which he holds. If held by the player called upon, it must be given him, and he calls again as before. If he fails to secure it, he takes one card from the pack and the call passes to the left. The player securing the most books wins the game. If all the cards are exhausted from a player's hand, he draws one from the pack. If the pack is exhausted, the players call from each other's hands only.

AUTHORS NO. 1

It will be observed that the pack is divided into four series of 13 cards each, A representing American prose writers; B American poets; C British prose writers and D British poets. Each series is numbered consecutively from 13 down to 1.

Deal six cards to each player and then turn up the top card of the pack. The authors of whatever series (A, B, C, D) this card represents are then said to be crowned, and the cards of that series have a greater value than of any other series. Thus if a card of series A is turned up all the cards of that series have a greater value than the cards of the other three and will take them in play. The turned up card is then placed at the centre of the pack which is placed in the centre of the table, face down.

The player at the dealer's left now leads a card and each in turn toward the left play a card on it. Each must play a card of the series led, if possible; if not can play a crowned card to take the play, or throw off a card of any uncrowned series as many be deemed advisable. The highest card played of the series led takes the play, unless one or more crowned cards have been played on it, in which case the highest crowned card takes it. The cards in each series rank from 13, highest to 1, lowest. The winner of the play then draws one card from the pack on the table, followed by each of the other players toward the left. Each hand will then again contain 6 cards as at the beginning of the game. The winner of the first play then leads to the next one and the game proceeds as before, each player drawing a card from the pack until the pack is exhausted after which the players play out the cards in their hands. The points each has made are then counted and scored, and the player to the left of the last dealer deals the cards as before. Points are scores as follows: Most cards, one point; most cards of crowned series, two points; most cards of any other series, one point; cards No. 13, 7 and 1 of the crowned series each score one point to the player taking them in. Fifteen points constitute a game. This may be played as a partnership game by two or three couples, if desired, the partners combining their scores.

AUTHORS NO. 2
This game represents a friend's rivalry, in which the American prose and poetical authors are allied as are also the British ones in an international contest. Deal 7 cards to each player, one at a time; then turn up the top card of the pack. Whatever series this cards represents is crowned as in game No. 1 with this difference, however, that when a series is crowned the highest card No. 13 of the allied series is crowned also and becomes the second highest in the pack, the No. 13 of the crowned series being the highest card. Thus if a card of series B is turned up, all the cards of series B are crowned and the No. 13 card only of series A is crowned also. B13 is then the highest in the pack, then A13 is next followed by B12, B11 etc. down to B1. The cards thus rank in value as follows, 1st No. 13 of the crowned series, No. 13 of the allied series, 3rd cards of the crowned series according to number, 12 being the highest, 11 next etc down to 1; 4th cards of the three uncrowned series according the number from 13 down to 1, except No. 13 of the allied series, which now belong to the crowned series.

The player at the left of the dealer begins by playing a card from his hand and each player to the left plays on it. If possible, each must play a card of the same series as led, if not he can play a crowned card to take the play, or may throw an unimportant card of any other series on it.

The highest card of the series takes the play, unless crowned cards have been placed on it, in which case the highest crowned card takes it. The winner of the play then leads a card, and each player to the left plays on it as before. When all the cards are played from the hands, the points are counted and a new deal is made, the deal passing to the left. Each play taken in scores one point, and eleven points constitute a game. In leading a high card of an uncrowned series should be leg, unless numerous high crowned cards are held, in which case the highest should be led.

AUTHORS NO. 3

Before beginning the game select a score keeper, who will keep count of all penalties inflicted against and points made by each player. Deal out all the cards one at a time, towards the left. The player at the dealer's left if he has a No. 7 card of any series, then plays it to the centre of the table. The next player if he has a No. 6 or 8 card of the same series as led, may play either alongside the No. 7 card; or if has another No 7 card he may play it below the first one played. The next player in turn may play another No. 7 card or may play a card of the next higher or lower number than any card on the table, building on top of the No. 6 card of each series down to No. 1 and on No 8 up to No. 13 (cards of the same series only being builded [spelling as shown] in the same pile). And so the play continues around the table to the left, each player endeavouring to build from his hand on to one of the piles on the table or start a new pile by playing a No. 7 card. If a player (including the leader at the start of the game) can not play a card from his hand, a penalty of one point is immediately scored against him by the score-keeper, this penalty being inflicted every time such player can not play when it is his turn to do so. The player first getting rid of all the cards from his hand is credited with one point for each card held in each of the other players' hands. When a player plays the last card from his hand, no more cards can be played, but all cards held at the time must be counted and one point for each card credited to the player who has played the last card. As soon as the scores have been properly credited to the winner, a new deal is had and the play proceeds as before. Twenty-five or fifty points constitute a game at the discretion of the players.

In case a player incurs a penalty and has no points to his credit from which to subtract such penalty, he is considered as owing the amount of such penalty or penalties, which amount must be subtracted from the first points he makes. A player will very frequently owe quite a number of points before he scores any to his credit. In case of two only desire to play, deal out the cards as if three were playing, allowing the third hand to lie on the table. Then each time either player plays a card from his hand, he draws one from this third hand until it is exhausted.

It was not unusual for a number of publishers to copy a successful game; sometimes quite blatantly. The first game of *Authors* was devised in 1861 by August Smith in the United States. Copyright laws did not exist until 1891 and legal actions were undertaken, but not always successfully. Over many years, companies were sold to others while some companies were amalgamated. In such cases, popular games were reissued by the new company.

Usually the authors represented are Louisa May Alcott, James Fenimore Cooper, Charles Dickens, Nathaniel Hawthorne, Washington Irving, Henry Wordsworth Longfellow, Edgar Allen Poe, Sir Walter Scott, William Shakespeare, Robert Lewis Stevenson, Alfred Lord Tennyson, William Makepeace Thackeray and Mark Twain. All were very well-known authors in the nineteenth century who remain well known.

The last of the major nineteenth-century card games still played today is *Snap*. John Jaques & Son Ltd introduced the game in England but it was probably based on another game by W. & S.B. Ives – *Memory*. There are forty-eight cards arranged in pairs, numbered 1 to 24, and each has a title. The theme is moral and each pair represents good and bad, such as vice/virtue. *Memory* and other card-matching games may be played with special cards or standard playing decks. Special cards may be smaller and any number of pairs may be used, depending on the number of players. The cards printed with coloured pictures, patterns or symbols are popular with young children. Rules for these games are like those for *Memory*, with players trying to get matching pairs. In the case of this particular set of cards, not only do the players need to remember the position of each but also the matching phrase which is not the same but the opposite.

This card game is for any number of players and is also called PELMANISM or CONCENTRATION.

It is easy to play and is an excellent test of memory and observation.

The playing area should be flat and as large as possible, the floor or a large table.

One player shuffles the cards and lays them face down on the table – in all directions and so that no card is touching another.

Each player tries to collect as many cards as possible by turning up pairs with the same rank or number.

The player to the left of the dealer starts the game. He turns over two cards at random and allows the other players to see them. If the two cards form a pair, he takes them and may turn over two more cards. He continues in this way until he turns over two cards that do not match. If the cards are turned over and do not match, the player must put them down in their original positions. His turn then ends.

The next player now turns over two cards. If the first card matches one that has already been turned over he must try to remember where that card is. If he is successful he takes the pair. He continues until he fails to turn over a matching pair.

Play continues with the players taking their turns in a clockwise direction, until all the cards have been collected.

The winner is the player with most cards at the end of the game.

A normal game of *Snap* relies on pictures, two cards having the same image. The game is simple enough for a young child to be able to play and yet rewarding enough for older children to enjoy, especially if it is accompanied by much noise. The cards are dealt out face down in front of the players. The first player turns over his top card followed by the second player. If the illustrations match, the first person to say SNAP wins the cards. The final winner is the one with the most pairs. The game can be played with forfeits, which are applied if the following person turns up a match, the first player must pay him a counter. The winner is the person with the most counters. To speed the game up, the players turn their card over at the same time and the person who notices two matching cards first will win them.

During the twentieth century, one of the best-known card games was actually a spelling game, *My Word, The Better Letter Game*. Several such games were published and the other famous one was *Lexicon*, published by Jaques & Son Ltd. Both of the 1930s, the games used letter cards to score.

My Word published by W.H. Storey & Co. Ltd of Croydon from the 1930s onward had an interesting introduction to its rules, which stated:

In presenting 'MY WORD' we feel we are bringing to you the ideal word making game, and one that will be enjoyed by every member of the family because of its differences for others of its class.

The Rules for 'MY WORD' are simple, and the method of scoring is such that players do NOT 'die out' and have to wait until the game ends before they can join in again.

In 'MY WORD' every player fights to the very end to increase his score.

In 'MY WORD' long waits (due to players having to study a large number of words) are eliminated as players are only concerned with ONE word at a time.

Further the object of 'MY WORD' is not solely to get rid of one's cards (as is usually the case) but rather to force up one's own score at the same time attempting to keep opponents' scores down.

The book of rules also has a page with a free offer. Apparently the public contacted the publishers with suggestions for other games that could be played with the cards. The publishers planned to test the games and compile a book of rules for the best ones.

The object of the game was for each player to add to or make words in such a way as to create the highest possible score while attempting to dispose of his cards. The game finished when one player had no cards left, however, the winner was the player with the highest score at the end of a complete game or *rubber*.[1] Words of less than three letters were not permitted, as were words extended by merely adding an 's'. Making plurals was only allowed if another letter besides the 's' was used. An example might be RACK to TRACKS, but not RACK to RACKS. As well as letter cards there were star cards, which were wild and could be added to make up or extend a word for more points. Two letter cards and star cards counted higher than single letter cards.[2]

The two letter cards have the letters one above the other and may be played in either sequence, for example, EN appears over NE so the word could be cENtre or NEw but a subsequent player may not reverse the order.[3] A two-letter card scores two points.

A one-star card may represent any one letter while a two-star card may only be two consecutive letters. A three-star card must represent three consecutive letters and by combining a one-star and three-star, four consecutive letters may be represented. With each combination the player must declare the letters represented however the next player, when adding to the word, may declare a new word.[4] However, using all stars to make a word is not allowed.

Play starts with the player to the left of the dealer. He must make a word and place it in the centre for all to see. If he cannot make a word from the cards in his hand he must either take the top card from the *reserve*, not seen, or the *turn-up* card. Play continues until one person has made a word. A card picked up is kept and no card is thrown away or placed in the *reserve* pile in its stead.

The next player after a word is made must either extend the word by adding cards anywhere in the word and/or at either end. He may instead box up the word[5] and start a new word from his hand. Otherwise he must take a card as before. Play continues until one player has finished his cards and he calls 'OUT'. A player is not compelled to either add to the existing word or place a new one down, but if he does neither of these things, he must collect a *reserve* or *turn-up* card.

Should a spelling be challenged and the player's word is wrongly spelt, he must take up the cards and play again *and* lose five points. If, however, the spelling is correct, the challenger loses five points. The scoring is simple. Each letter or star earns a point (double and treble for more letters and stars per card). When a player extends a word, the whole word is scored, not just the added letters. When a player declares 'OUT', all the players' scores are calculated, with points deducted for any cards still held.

Dissected and Jigsaw Puzzles

A puzzle is a mystery to be solved. Whether it is conundrum, modern-day *Sudoku*, or a jigsaw, concentration is needed to bring about a successful conclusion. Jigsaw puzzles and their predecessor, the dissected puzzle, have remained constant favourites for all ages for more than 200 years. Puzzles can be a solitary and quiet activity but it is surprising that few people can resist stopping to help fit in a piece or two as they pass.

Those publishers already famous for their board and card games also produced puzzles. In the eighteenth century, engravings were hand-coloured then mounted on thin wood board, often made of mahogany. The same or similar images were used for the puzzles as for the board games and the subjects were the same – geography, history and morals. The first puzzles were cut by a small handsaw and were referred to as dissections. Jigsaws were introduced in the mid-nineteenth century and replaced the handsaw for cutting the puzzles, hence the name jigsaw puzzle. In the twentieth century, as cardboard replaced wood, mass production took effect and the puzzles were cut by machine. The normal pattern has six different interlocking shapes and the machines stamped them out, sheet by sheet.

A Londoner by the name of John Spilsbury is accredited with the first dissected puzzles designed for children. He was listed as an engraver and map dissector in wood, 'in order to facilitate the teaching of geography'. Producing about thirty different maps, each one was mounted on thin mahogany, cut around the obvious boundaries, boxed up and sold for a child to reassemble. The boundaries were the counties for a map of England and Wales, the countries or principalities of Europe and whole countries or areas of the known world. Spilsbury also produced and sold many printed items, books, maps and even silk handkerchiefs. When he died in 1769, it was a few years before any other publisher took up the idea of puzzles. It may have been too labour intensive as each was hand-cut. However, in the 1780s publishers took the idea of the dissected maps and added other subjects, not all of them obvious puzzle material.

The early dissection had interlocking pieces only on the outer edges, to hold the puzzle together with the rest of the pieces abutting. In some cases, it was necessary to place the interlocking key shapes into their eyeholes either from above or from below as the cuts sloped and the eyeholes would only accept the key at the angle of the cut.

The inner pieces had wavy lines and in many cases were very similar to each other. The child would need to learn or recognise the subject of each piece in order to place it in the correct position. *Engravings for Teaching the Elements of English History and Chronology, after the manner of dissected maps for teaching geography* was published in London 'as the act directs July 1st 1787 by Carrington Bowles, St Paul's Church Yard, C. Dilly Poultry and W. Darton, Birchin Lane', who is said to be the sculptor of the engraving. It shows the portraits and short biographies of monarchs from William I to George II with historical notes about their reigns. It includes the death of George II but no mention or details of his successor. The abbreviations in the texts are detailed and the directions show the purposes of the puzzle.

> Learn to put the heads together in succession.
> Get the dates in the ovals and houses of the respective kings.
> Learn the names of the principal personages of each reign separately.
> Get by heart the historical and chronological facts of the respective reigns with the dates of battles, treaties etc.

By the early nineteenth century, many subjects, pictorial as well as factual, were dissected. The great industrial strides of the century were reflected, the railway, ship building, even the Great Exhibition of 1851. Some retained the moral aspects and illustrated happier events or subjects, such as *My Mother* with poems from *Original Poems for Infants' Minds*. The child assembling the puzzle would be encouraged to read the poems aloud.

William Darton, Edward Wallis, John Passmore and William Peacock produced many puzzles between them. For the first half of the century hand-coloured engravings and etchings were prominent, gradually being replaced with lithographs and then chromolithographs, those printed in colours. Maps continued to be printed and some were very detailed giving shipping routes, roads and railways. The double dissection was introduced showing a map on one side and a picture on the reverse.

In the twentieth century jigsaw puzzles followed the trends already set, they reflected the world around them. Maps continued, some with more interesting subjects such as including a country's flag. Others with cut-out space into which would be inserted the name of the country's capital or principal towns. As with other games of the period, war did influence the subjects chosen as did the Royal Family.

Coronations and the two young princesses generated many puzzles, including some of the first that were sold for charitable causes. Puzzles were created for different age groups with different levels of ability. Large bright pictures made of six pieces for the very young child became 5,000-piece sets for the older child and adult.

In the 1930s, Chad Valley Co Ltd introduced a series on behalf of the Great Western Railway, GWR. These puzzles showed the towns and the countryside together with famous landmarks where the railway travelled. The Cunard Line had Chad Valley publish a set of pictures of their ships while the company reached an agreement with Walt Disney and published a number of puzzles based on the Mickey Mouse cartoon character. Nursery rhymes, popular children's songs, poems and book characters led to a great number of puzzles by many of the major publishers of the century. Raphael Tuck & Sons Ltd produced a series based on *The Little Grey Rabbit* and Journet of London produced a number of special puzzles that required magnetism or made a three-dimensional shape.

Raphael Tuck & Sons Ltd was a well-known printing company of many toys and stationery sundries and in 1914 the company acquired Bacon's Reversible Zigsaw Puzzles, Zig-Zag Co. and Zag-Zaw Puzzles. The puzzles had few interlocking pieces and the pieces were designed in the shape of recognisable shapes such as household utensils, animals and letters of the alphabet, which fitted together to form a picture. A guide picture rarely accompanied the puzzles and a large one could take many hours of concentration to complete. This type of puzzle was found to be easy for making at home, as the pieces did not need the accuracy of interlocking and holding together.

During the years of war, both the First World War (1914–18) and the Second World War (1939–45), the companies producing jigsaw puzzles turned their talents to the war machine. Nevertheless, jigsaws were important recreational aids for military men of all the Services as well as the general population.

As the century progressed, jigsaw puzzles continued and are as popular today as ever. Space and moon landings added pictures to be assembled and there has been a craze for the abstract idea, a picture of marbles or jelly beans, and shapes in black and white. Three-dimensional puzzles have also been introduced, in the shape of a globe of the world, or a building. These are not for everyone and the picture postcard country cottage remains as popular as ever. There are clubs, which trade puzzles, and schools where simple puzzles are used to teach arithmetic and spelling.

Glossary

A few of the words used in the instructions of the games can be confusing as over the long period of time their meanings or their shapes have changed. Before starting any new game, it is essential that all the players understand the rules. If the players are making their own rules or adapting set rules, again it is essential that they all understand them.

TEETOTUM or TOTUM
This is a spinning top used as a replacement for dice. During the eighteenth and nineteenth centuries, publishers and parents felt that dice were a bad influence on children. Dice were found in most homes for use by adults only. The teetotum may have as many as twelve sides depending on the game being played but the normal was four, six or eight sides. In the early years, teetotums were made of bone and occasionally of ivory. By the mid-nineteenth century, it became a spinner with a wooden post and a cardboard disc. Even now, some games are issued with a cardboard disc for use with a pencil.

DIE and DICE

A single die or two dice may be used in any game. The dice determine the play, how far markers are moved. Occasionally one die will be the standard one to six spots version while the other has different markings or colours and guided the players to take actions above and beyond the forward movement. By the end of the nineteenth century, dice were in common use for children's games, gone were the worries about children being corrupted.

Some games do not use the square dice, they may use stick dice, long rectangular shapes marked to differentiate them. Other games may use cowrie shells or triangular shapes.

POOL or KITTY

However much publishers and parents were worried about the evils of dice, they had no trouble about the gambling element introduced with a Pool. Most eighteenth- and early nineteenth-century games had a Pool as the ultimate goal to be won. Every player had to pay a set amount at the start into it and it received and paid out rewards and forfeits throughout a game. Few modern games have a Pool now, *Monopoly* being one of the exceptions with its Bank, although the Bank is not won at the end of the game.

MARKERS

Markers are referred to by many names. They are the playing pieces on the board which are moved. They mark a player's position. Some games such as *Chess* refer to markers as MEN, others such as *Monopoly* as TOKENS. Some of the early travelling games referred to markers as TRAVELLERS.

COUNTERS

Usually when games refer to counters, they mean discs that are used in addition to the markers. Often counters are the tokens used to put in the Pool or to give and receive as forfeits and rewards. However, there are games such as *Go* that use small discs as the markers.

REWARDS and FORFEITS
Many early games were played using rewards and forfeits. The Rewards could be an extra turn, forward movement or receiving of a counter from another player or the Pool. Forfeits could be waiting one or more than one turn, backward movement or the payment to other players or the Pool. Some forfeits were very harsh. Occasionally a player had to leave the game entirely or spend a lot of his time in jail with costly payments for release.

IT
The person who is the chaser in a game of *Tag* may have other names but generally the phrase is: 'You're IT'.

Notes

Chapter 1: Games with Little or No Equipment

1   A variation on *Pass the Parcel* was *Passing the Button*. In this game, the players keep their hands in a prayer position. A button is in the first player's hands and passed around or not as the player decides by placing his hands over the hands of the next person. It is up to the rest of the players to decide where the button is. The person who holds the button at the end of the round retires from the game.

2   A mechanical game entitled *Simon Says* was issued in 1978 by the American manufacturer Milton Bradley. At a time when personal computers were very new and certainly not in every home, this game was a round, battery-operated device marked with four coloured shapes. When operated, sounds were emitted and the players were invited to repeat longer and longer combinations of tones which they had to duplicate by striking the coloured shapes. The game was said to challenge both visual and hearing memory.

3   'But there is one kind of small toy which I have forgotten to mention, yet which every schoolboy dearly cherishes-toys which lie so snugly in his pocket that he can handle them all unnoticed, even in school hours, and that our girls can amuse themselves with in many a pleasant game of solitaire. Of course I mean marbles, things which, like pins, are for ever being bought and lost; things that neither melt nor break, but simply vanish no one knows where, never to be seen or heard of again. Some

are of glass, but the greater number of these little treasures are made of a hard stone found near Coburg, in Saxony. The stone is first broken with a hammer into small cubical fragments, and about one hundred or one hundred and fifty of these are ground at one time in a mill somewhat resembling a flour-mill. The lower stone – which remain at rest – has several concentric and circular grooves; the upper stone is of the same diameter as the lower, and is made to revolve by water or other power. Minute streams of water are directed into the furrows of the lower stone. The pressure of the water on the little pieces rolls them over in all directions, and in about a quarter of an hour the whole of the rough fragments are reduced to nearly one size; they are afterwards smoothed and stained, and sold by the sackful, to be retailed by pennyworths.' Excerpt taken from *The Wonderland of Work* by C.L. Matéaux and published by Cassel, Petter, Galpin & Co., London, Paris & New York, about 1880.

Chapter 2: Games for One or More Players

1   'The games were designed by our in-house team, and in this instance specifically by Justine Cardy. We have a huge ideas bank of new products being worked on constantly, and around 4 to 6 of these ideas are turned into full products for launch each year. *The Giant Connect 4* was developed in 2005, and the *Giant Dominoes* in 2004. They are a part of a range of outdoor games, some giant versions of classic games, and some specifically designed to work on an outdoor scale.

The *Giant Dominoes* are made from wood; hand finished, and are packed in wooden storage box. The *Giant Connect 4* is made from plastic, to make it as hard wearing as possible. We also have a wooden version, called *Big 4*, but this is not as hard wearing and does not perform so well in the wet, so is more suitable for indoor use.'

Chapter 5: Games for Juveniles of 'Both Sexes'

1   The playing sheet is lettered in the lower-left corner, over Morocco and Algeria with the following comment. 'NB In Africa the human mind seems degraded below its natural state, to dwell long upon the manners of this country, a country so immers'd in rudeness and barbarity, (besides that it could afford little instruction) would be disgusting to every lover of mankind. The inhabitants of Africa are deprived at present of all arts

and sciences, by which the human mind remains torpid and inactive, a gloomy sameness every where prevails, and the trifling distinctions which are discovered among them, seem rather to arise from an excess of brutality on the one hand, than any perceptible approaches towards refinement on the other.'

2   The authors of the descriptions needed to explain why Alexandria was included when it was not a British Dominion. Their explanation is as follows:

'Alexandria does not properly come within the limits of notice by this little work, the British nation having no possessions here: but, as the traveller to India by what is called the overland route, necessarily disembarks at this port, it appears desirable to make some mention of it. It was founded by Alexander the Great; and the trade to the East being at that time carried on by way of the Mediterranean, Alexandria, from its situation, became the emporium of that trade, and was for a long period the centre of commerce, learning and civilisation. The discovery of a passage to India by way of the Cape, was a severe blow to the prosperity of Alexandria; and, from the combination of a variety of causes, it gradually degenerated into a mere fishing village. Mahomed Ali, the late Viceroy of Egypt, did much for its restoration; and since the Peninsular and Oriental company have run their steamers to Egypt, Alexandria has still further increased in importance.'

3   Four statements involving the slavery show the feelings of the publishers shortly after the abolition:

No. 4. SIERRA LEONE

… increasing both in prosperity and population, the later being from time to time augmented by the cargoes of captured slave-ships, brought here for adjudication (a court being established for this purpose), the kidnapped negroes from condemned ships being here set at liberty …

No. 23, FALKLAND ISLANDS. DIRECTIONS FOR PLAY

As there is little here of interest to detain the traveller, he is at liberty to proceed to No. 25. (Guiana), and witness the cultivation of cotton by free blacks.

No. 28. JAMAICA

The third largest of the West India islands, was discovered by Columbus in 1494. The Spaniards formed a settlement here in 1509, and treated the natives with great cruelty. It was taken by the English in 1656, and was cultivated by the aid of negro slaves until the year 1834, when slavery was happily abolished throughout the British dominions …

Spin again to commemorate the abolition of Negro slavery throughout the British dominions.

No. 32. CANADA (North America)

… and the soil is even more fertile, affording great encouragement to the industry of the many thousands who annually leave their native country for this less crowded spot. We may also rejoice in this land furnishing a place of refuge to many negro slaves, who have the happiness to escape from cruel bondage in the United States, and who, once setting their foot on these shores, are beyond the power of the man-hunter.

4   The full list on this exciting travel through Asia does not do justice to the descriptions given for each. Some of the spellings are now very strange but were the accepted forms at the time. However, under No. 9 the player must note that there were three different accepted spellings for the word 'fakiers'.

1. Skeleton of Mammoth and Samoyeds
2. Kamtschadale Travelling
3. Tartar catching a Horse
4. Russian Exile in Siberia
5. Hunting in India
6. Chinese making Tea
7. Japanese Captive sending his Picture to his Wife, and Sword to his Son, as a token of his intention to commit suicide
8. Giving a Chinese Boy his first Cap
9. Fakiers in India
10. Battle between the British and Indian
11. Missionary Preaching
12. Widow Burning Herself
13. The four Casts
14. One Grand Lama lying dead, & an Infant exalted as his Substitute
15. Jaggernaut
16. A Turkish Caravan attacked by Arabs
17. Pilgrimage to Mecca
18. Guebres, or Worshippers of Fire surprised by Mohatmetans of Persia
19. A Circassian being sold
20. Portrait of a Circassian
21. Portrait of a Chinese
22. Portrait of a Baschkir
23. Portrait of a Persian
24. Portrait of a Turk
25. Portrait of a Gentoo

5   The text is very critical of sights of cruelty, bondage and slavery and emphasises the development of the anti-slavery laws. Equally the author of the game was very distressed by the suicide of the Japanese, who he

felt was above that method of death. There are a further seven notes to
be read out under direction in the game. These do give some background
details to particular events or ideas from a strictly British view point.

6   Occasionally a game is published that would now not be considered
suitable. In the 1950s, Prestige Toys of America published Uranium
Rush. It was based on the Federal Government's offer of $10,000 to
prospectors who found workable uranium claims. The game included a
Geiger counter which lit up.

Chapter 6: History Made Easy

1   (Sample of the texts to be read.)

'No. 51. Britain seems to have been little known before its invasion
by the Romans under Julius Caesar. At the fall of their empire it was
divided among a number of native independent princes; one of whom,
Vortigern, being perpetually harassed by the Picts and Scots, invited the
Saxons to his assistance. These perfidious allies, however, soon turned
their arms against, and nearly extirpated the Britons, founding in the
country seven distinct kingdoms, called the Saxon Heptarchy, which,
AD 827, were all united under Egbert, the first king of England. About
the year 887, the Danes became masters of the whole country, obliged
King Alfred to conceal himself from their pursuit, and continued to
govern the kingdom till the death of Hardicanute, AD 1041, when
the Saxon line was restored in the person of Edward the Confessor.
This prince dying without issue, Harold, the son of Earl Goodwin,
ascended the throne; but his right was disputed by William, duke of
Normandy, who, landing at Hastings with 60,000 men, slew Harold,
and obtained possession of the kingdom. The Norman line continued
till 1154, when Henry II, first king of the house of Plantagenet, assumed
the sovereignty; in whole reign the conquest of Ireland was achieved.
Henry IV was the first of the Lancastrian line, and his son Henry V was,
by right of marriage, publicly crowned King of France. In the reign of
Henry VI was begun that dreadful war between the houses of York and
Lancaster, which eventually established the former on the throne, in the
person of Edward IV. Henry VII established the line of Tudor, which
continued till James I, of the line of Stuart, by whom the kingdoms of
England and Scotland were united. The barbarous massacre of Charles I,
AD 1649 occasioned an interregnum under Oliver Cromwell, and
Richard, his son: but, at the end of eleven years, Charles II son of the
late monarch, was called to the throne. The bigoted attachment of his

successor, James II, to the Church of Rome, occasioned his deposition:
when William, Prince of Orange, and Mary, daughter of the late king,
were jointly proclaimed. The reign of Anne, sister to Mary, the last
queen, continued till 1714, when George, the first of that name, and
the house of Brunswick, assumed the crown. He was succeeded by his
son, George II, whose prosperous reign was embellished by the most
signal victories, and continued thirty-three years: when his illustrious
grandson, George III, ascended the throne.'

2   RULES FOR PLAYING THE GAME

1.   The players are provided with a Card, containing nine Letters, nine
     Numbers, two Crosses and one Blank, which are to be cut up on the
     lines with a pair of scissors.

2.   The letters are to be distributed one to each player, according to the
     number about to play, and the remainder laid aside. They are used
     to mark each player's position in the Game.

3.   The numbers, crosses and black are to be placed in a lady's reticule,
     and drawn in turn, one by each player, after the manner of a lottery.

4.   Each player, on drawing a number, is to place his letter on the same
     number in the Game, and read the description aloud. When it is
     his turn to draw another, he adds them together and advances his
     letter to that number which they make when so added, reading as
     before, and observing any directions which may be given him. But
     if he draw a cross, he is to draw again, till he obtain a number, which
     number is to be deducted from, instead of added to his former
     station, and his letter moved back accordingly. Each card to be
     returned to the bag after drawing.

5.   Whoever draws a blank, remains at his former number.

6.   After each player has drawn once, the Game is to be continued in
     the same manner, passing the bag round, till some one makes up the
     exact number 151, who wins the Game.

7.   If a player go beyond No. 151, he must go as many back as he had
     exceeded it, and the lottery must continue till some one makes up
     the exact number.

8.   If two players arrive at the same number, the one who arrived last
     must go back to his former number.

9.   When a player is sent back to any place, he is not to read the
     description, or attend to the directions in italics, and when sent
     forward he is only to read the description and stop there till his turn
     to draw again.

3   SCIENCE IN SPORT OR THE PLEASURES OF ASTRONOMY
     A NEW GAME REVISED AND APPROVED BY MRS BRYAN

BLACKHEATH, LONDON. PRINTED FOR E. WALLIS 42
SKINNER STREET, SNOW HILL BY T. DAVIS 117 MINORIES.
THE LAWS OF THE GAME

1. Each player must have a pyramid and four counters of the same colour.
2. The first player is to be determined by spinning the teetotum; the highest spinner to be the first player etc.
3. The first player must read the introduction aloud before he begins to play.
4. The first player is to spin and according to the number turned up on the teetotum, he is to place his pyramid: thus if he turns up 3, he is to place his pyramid at No. 3.
5. After the first player has spun, the rest are to spin in the order determined by Law 2.
6. The number turned up at each spinning is to be added on to that on which the players' pyramid stands: thus if a player whose pyramid stands on No. 3, spins and the teetotum turns up 4, he must place his pyramid at No. 7 and so on till some one arrives at 35, who wins the game.
7. If the last spin does not exactly make up 35, but goes beyond it, the player is to go back as many as he exceeds that number and try his fortune again till some one arrives at the lucky number.
8. When a player is to stop one or more turns, he must place as many counters as he is to stop turns on the number he arrives at and when his turn of spinning comes he is to take up a counter instead of spinning and so on until they are all redeemed, when he may proceed.

    Introductory Observations are engraved on the playing sheet.

    *First published by John Wallis in 1804 and reissued by Edward Wallis. The thirty-five squares have portraits of astronomers and representations of astronomical phenomena. At the time, nine planets and their movements around the sun were known. Intermingled with facts are compartments dealing with fiction (the Man in the Moon), behaviour (the Studious Boy and the Blockhead), signs of the Zodiac, comets and rainbows, and astronomers.

4   No. 37 THE LION

This strong, fierce, yet noble-looking animal, is produced in Africa and the hottest parts of Asia. In the scorching deserts of Zaara and Bilidalgerid he reigns sole master of the desolate regions. His rage is tremendous, his courage undaunted; but, when approaching the habitation of man, his ferocity seems abated: caution, and even timidity, succeed. He seems conscious of the power of his enemy; and, once acquainted with him and the nature of his arms, he loses his natural fortitude, and becomes terrified at his voice. When under the control of a keeper, they are wonderfully tame, and will permit of much freedom: nor do they resent ill-treatment, like many other animals, though some severe instances of retaliation have occurred. There is cruelty in irritating even a wild beast; and we can feel little pity for those who bring upon themselves a punishment so fatal. The form of the Lion is majestic: his large and shaggy mane, which he erects at pleasure, surrounding his awful front; his huge eye-brows, round and fiery eyes, his formidable teeth, present a terrific though noble object to our view. The length of the largest is from eight to nine feet, the tail about four. The female is about one-fourth less, and without a mane, which in the lion grows longer and thicker as he advances in years. Nothing can be more dreadful that [sic] the roaring of the lion in his native wilds. It is said they are rapidly decreasing; and we may well spare a race so terrific. Many instances have been adduced to prove the lion's forbearance towards its victim, particularly when greatly inferior to itself in strength.

Chapter 7: Morals

1   THE COTTAGE OF CONTENT OR, RIGHT ROADS AND
     WRONG WAYS.
     Description of the Game.
         The Game is played with a Teetotum and Travellers for the Players.
     The object is to reach the 'COTTAGE OF CONTENT', which is attained
     by moving along the Roads from the 'Starting Post', circle by circle, as
     each player may be directed after spinning the Teetotum and turning up
     the direction he is to take. Each circle is in the centre of four roads, and
     is marked with the letters, F. R. L. B., indicating Forward, Right, Left,
     Backward. The letter F points the road to the next circle Forward, and
     the other letters point to the directions Right, Left and Backward. When
     the player has spun the Teetotum, he is to move his Traveller to the next
     circle from him, either Forward, Right, Left or Backward, as the letter he
     turns up may indicate. This is continued till a player wins the GAME by
     arriving at the 'COTTAGE OF CONTENT'.
     RULES
     1.   Draw lots who shall play first, second, third, etc and let each player
          take his Traveller accordingly.
     2.   Any number can play the Game at the same time, each being
          provided with Counters for forfeits. On the commencement of a
          Game, each player is to put three Counters into the pool.

3. The first player begins the Game, by spinning the Teetotum and moving his Traveller from the 'Starting Post' along the road to the first circle on the right, on the left or the circle figured No. 1 on the road, forward, according as the Teetotum may turn up. At the Starting Post, if the Teetotum turn up B, the Player cannot move, but waits his turn to spin again.

4. The second player then spins the Teetotum, and moves along to the first circle on either of the roads, as the Teetotum may turn up. He is followed by the other players in rotation. When the players moving from the 'Starting Post' find the circle they are directed to occupied by another player, they remove the possessor, except the occupier of the circle figured No. 1, and take his place. The player thus removed will renew the Game from the 'Starting Post' when it is his turn again to spin the Teetotum.

5. When all the players have spun, the first player then spins again, and moves his Traveller according to the letter the Teetotum turns up; and the same is continued by each player spinning in rotation, and moving accordingly.

6. When a player is directed along a road, on which the circle next to him is already occupied by another player, the two players are to change places.

7. When a player is so directed that he meets with 'No Thoroughfare', he cannot move, but waits his turn to spin again.

8. Every time a player passes along a road that requires a forfeit, he is to pay the demand, although he has been along the road before. When a player is removed along a forfeit-road, by another displacing him, it is required for the player only who causes the removal to pay the forfeit. The same rule is to apply likewise to the payments that are to be taken from the Pool.

9. The Player who first reaches 'THE COTTAGE OF CONTENT' by being directed Forward when at the next circle to the Cottage on any one of the three roads which lead to the entrance, wins the Game and takes the contents of the Pool.

Chapter 9: Monopoly and Cluedo

1 In the game illustrated, the markers are a ship, a car, a dog, a boot, a hat and an iron.

2 The players are allotted £1,500 each, divided into two £500, four £100, one £50, one £20, two £10, one £5 and five £1 notes.

3   The introduction to the rules states that the board represents the ground-floor plan of 'Tudor Close'. The object is to solve by means of elimination and deduction the problem of the mysterious murder of Dr Black, the owner of the house, whose body has been found at the foot of the stairs leading to the cellars at a spot marked X.

4   The playing pieces are appropriately coloured to match the names of the suspects: Col. Mustard – yellow, Prof. Plum – purple, The Rev. Green – green, Mrs Peacock – blue, Miss Scarlet – red and Mrs White – white.

5   A cab may be taken from the Carriage Depot to any other location on the board. This is instead of a throw of the die. Here, a player may if he wishes check the clue in which case he does not move until his next turn. However, if he does not wish to check the clue, he may move immediately to his chosen location and check the clue there.

6   Scotland Yard Cards may be used to seal off a location a player has entered in order to keeps the others out. The card is placed over the entrance when the player leaves. However, 221B Baker Street, Scotland Yard and the Locksmiths are not lockable and the rules advise that a player may not seal a location if another player is still in it. The docks and the park have more than one entrance, but only one may be blocked at a time.

    Players are entitled to hold one such card. If it is used they may go to Scotland Yard and collect another one, as well as look for a clue.

7   The Skeleton Key Cards are used to open a sealed location. Both cards are then returned to the respective holding locations, either Scotland Yard or the Locksmiths.

    Players are entitled to hold one such card. If it is used they may go to the Locksmiths and collect another one, as well as look for a clue.

8   When a player moves into a location, he is entitled to look at the clue which corresponds with that location, however, at any time during the game, a player may read the Case adventure again.

    There are two types of clues and these are listed in the booklet. The first type is a general statement which gives a fact or facts about the case being played. The second is a puzzle clue which is often a syllable clue to a certain item – the killer or criminal, the weapon, the motive, the hiding place, the cause of death or a code. These have more than one part to them and all the relevant clues must be sought before the answer is found. As the killer clues may spell out a name, the person may be deemed the murderer. Not all the games have killers for example as the one cited here.

Chapter 10: Spelling

1. The players' markers are quite different to many games of this type. The players are asked to select one which they feel reflects their personality. The coloured markers are marked with drawings of symbols: clef – entertaining, exclamation mark – dynamic, pound sign – generous, question mark – thoughtful, percentage sign – 1 in 100 and a floral 'Dingbat' sign.

2. *Totally Dingbats* has within the rules what is termed 'The Players' Roles': On your turn, you are the Solver. You will roll both dice, move your playing piece and try to solve a Dingbat, a Kingbat or a Thingbat. The player on your right will be your Moderator. The Moderator draws the card you must solve, looks at the solutions, times you and judges your answers. In some instances, other players may try to solve the card by competing with you. The black, specially-marked die indicates if you play SOLO, with ONE other player or with ALL other players.

   The rules continue with 'What the Moderator Does' which includes secretly looking at the solution of the card and flipping the timer over so the countdown begins. The Moderator is also the judge and listens to players' guesses and decides if anyone has solved the card. He must also decide whether a guess is close enough to be deemed correct.

Chapter 11: Card Games

1. A *rubber* was a set of games allowing the players to all have a turn as the dealer. For example, if there were four players, four, eight or twelve games would make a *rubber*.

2. Each player receives ten cards. The remaining cards, called the *reserve*, are placed face down with the top card face up and placed to the side. This card is given the name *turn-up*. Whenever a player takes this card, the next in the pile is turned face up.

3. The example given in the rules booklet has the start word cAR/RAt scores five. The next player inserts a *C and adds uRE/ER to make the word cAR*CatuRE (caricature) for ten points.

4. The example given in the rules booklet has the start word st**d, declared stand. The next player adds E to make st**ed and declares stored. The third player adds K to make st**ked and declares stacked.

5. To box up a word means to collect the cards in a haphazard manner and place them face down under the *reserve* pile. Only one word at a time is being played. If a player wishes not to add to an existing word, he boxes it up and starts his own word.

Illustrations

1   NOUVEAU JEU DE L'OIE REGLES

Il faut d'abord convenir de ce qu'on veit jouer et payer aux reencounters et accidents. Ce jeu est composé de nombres depuis 1 jusqu'à 63, et le premier qui atteint ce nombre final où est le jardin de l'Oie gagne la partie, mais on n'y'arrive pas facilement. Pour jouer à ce jeu, il faut avoir deux dez que chaque joueur jetter une fois, il comptera sur le jeu le nombre de points qu'il aura fait, et mettra sa marque sur le nombre amené; chaque joueur aura une marque diferente afin de la reconnaitre. On ne peuf prendre pied sure les Oies que sont placées aux Nos. 5, 9, 14, 18, 23, 27, 32, 36, 41, 45, 50, 54, et 59.

Celui que fera 9 par 5 et 4 ira au No. 53 où sont figures deux dez. Celui qui fera 9 par 6 et 3 ira au No. 26 ou sont également deux dez. Celui qui du premier coup fera 6 où est le pont chinois, payer le prix convenu et ira au No. 12 se noyer sous le pont. Celui qui arrivera au No. 19 où se trouve use Hotellerie, payera le prix convenu et y restera jusqu'à ce que chacun des autres joueurs ait joué 2 coups. Celui qui arrivera au No. 31 où est représenté le Puits d'amour payera le prix convenu et y restera jusqu'à ce qu'un des joueurs amenant le même point vienne l'en retirer, alors il se transportera à la place de celui qui l'aura délivré. Celui qui arrivera au No. 42 où est le Labyrinthe payera le prix convenu et retournera au No. 30. Celui qui arrivera au No. 52 où est la Prison, payera le prix accordé et y restera renfermé jusqu'à ce qu'un autre vienne l'en refirer. Celui qui arrivera au No. 58 où est le Corbillard recommencera tout le jeu et payera le prix convenu. Celui qui sera recontré par us autre payera le prix convenu et prendra la place que vient de quitter celui qui le rencontre. Si en approchant du No. 63 on fait plus de points qu'il n'en faut pour y arriver juste on retourne en arrière d' autant de points que ce qu'on a de trop.

2   This particular game board comprises sixty-three squares placed in an oval design with the rules in the centre. At each corner is an illustration of boys playing games: lower-left – billiards, lower-right – ninepin bowling, upper-left – marbles and upper-right – on a swing. Thirteen squares show illustrations of geese, as does the final square, No. 63, that is entitled the 'Garden of the Goose'. Animals, both real and mythical, are shown such as a goat and dragon, as well as real and mythical people, a sculptor and angels for example. The rules are the same as any other game of the Goose with penalties in the payments and backward movement and rewards in the receipt of payments for forward movement.

3   RULES FOR PLAYING
1.   This game is played with a Teetotum marked on 6 sides, and any number of persons may play.
2.   Each player must be provided with two dozen counters, (which, before playing they may value as they please), and a coloured one for a mark. At the beginning of the game each player must put 6 into the pool.
3.   Spin for first player and whoever spins the highest number must begin the game.
4.   Whatever number you spin, place your mark on the number; and if it be a print, refer to the explanation. When it is your turn to spin again, add the two numbers together and move on accordingly. (For example, if the first spin is 6 move to No. 6 and if the second spin is 3, add this to the 6 and move to No. 9.)
5.   Whoever spins a Golden Egg takes a counter from the pool; but if you spin a blank, put one in.
6.   If two players arrive at the same number, he that was there first is to move back to the place the last player left, from whom he is to receive 2 for resigning his place.
7.   Whoever arrives at the exact number (33) first, wins the game; but if by spinning, he goes beyond that number, he must move twice as many back as he exceeds it.

References to the Game:
1.   Mother Goose mounted on a gander – Pay 4 to secure her favour.
3.   Mother Goose's Retreat.
5.   Colin receiving the goose from Mother Goose, who tells him to give the Egg to Avaro, Colinette's father. Take Up 2.
7.   Colin shows the golden egg to Avaro who wants him to kill the goose, that he may give him all the eggs at once, before he marries Colinette.
9.   Colin, having ungratefully consented to kill the goose presented him by his best friend, is changed by Mother Goose to Harlequin, and Colinette to Columbine. Pay 3 for Ingratitude.
11. The mock dance between the Clown and Harlequin, dressed as a Barrow woman. Stay 1 turn to see this.
13. The Clown and Pantaloon (formerly Avaro) coming to an Inn, they sit down to supper with the Landlord, when Harlequin enters and causes the chairs and tables to ascend with them, while he and Columbine sit down quietly to their supper, laughing at the situation of the others. Before they can get down you may move on to No. 18.

15. The Clown and Pantaloon entering in pursuit of Harlequin and Columbine, the former is caught in a steel trap while a spring gun goes off and frightens Pantaloon, who leads off the Clown by the leg. Pay 2 to have your wound cured.

17. Harlequin and Columbine, to elude pursuit, place themselves as the two well-known figures at St Dunstan's church, striking the bell. Take up 4 for this ingenious thought.

19. Vauxhall Gardens, where the Clown gains admission by appearing as a Pandean Minstrel, playing on a fish kettle with a ladle and whisk, with his chin resting on a hair broom. Stay two turns to see the amusements of the place and laugh at this curious figure.

21. The clown steals a letter from the Post Office, containing a bank note, which he pockets; then another in which he finds a small cord and the words 'Sir, I'll trouble you for a line'. For this knavish trick pay 3.

23. The Clown, attempting to drink out of a bottle, finds himself disappointed by the bottom always presenting itself to his lips. You must be disappointed by going back to No. 14.

25. Harlequin pours wine from his sword into the mouth of the Odd Fish. For this act of humanity take up 6.

27. Odd fish, in gratitude to Harlequin, dives into the sea after the golden egg, which he presents to his benefactor.

29. Harlequin restores the golden egg to Mother Goose, who is at length pacified. Having made some amends for your fault, take up two.

31. Harlequin and Columbine united by Mother Goose in a submarine palace, the dwelling of Odd Fish. This being a most beautiful scene, you may stay one turn to admire it.

33. An exact representation of Mother Goose mounted on her favourite gander. By her permission you are allowed to take all the fish remain in the pool and are declared the winner of this game.

NB If the players are inclined for another game, the winner of the first to begin it now.

Game shows episodes and characters from the pantomime of the same title, including the Clown and Harlequin and places in London including St Dunstan's church and Vauxhall Gardens. Published at the height of Grimaldi the Clown's career, who is featured in compartment twenty-one, much of the game is taken up with the rules and the number of compartments is reduced to thirty-three, of which seventeen are illustrated, each having its own story and reward or forfeit. Half the remaining compartments show a golden egg, which if landed on has a reward of one counter; the other half, which are blank, carry a forfeit of one counter.

4   EXPLANATION OF THE GAME

Having a box and a pair of dice, each person who plays should be furnished with a dozen counters, the value of which is to be agreed on and when the Amusement is over for the night, each person is to be accountable for the same, those who want more must buy a winner. Each person should also be furnished with another counter with the initial of his/her name thereon (or any other letter judged most proper for distinction) which is to be placed over the number thrown and moved agreeable to the following rules:

NB Paying a fine of 1, 2, 3 is meant so many counters and by 1 or 2 months is meant the person must wait 'till the box has passed him so many times.

RULES OF THE GAME

1. Whoever comes to the Water No 6 must pay one for being ferried over and go to No. 10.
2. Whoever arrives at the Inn No 9 must pay one for taking refreshments and go to No. 12.
3. Whoever possesses Piety, Honesty, Sobriety, Gratitude, Prudence, Truth, Chastity, Sincerity, Humility, Industry, Charity, Humanity, Generosity is entitled to advance six towards the Mansion of Happiness.
4. Whoever posses Audacity, Cruelty, Immodesty or Ingratitude must return to his former situation, till his turn comes to throw again and not even think of happiness much less partake of it.
5. Poverty, the Whipping Post, Bridewell, the Pillory, the Stocks, Newgate, and Ruin are to be considered as blanks in your progress to the Mansion: for it would be cruel to punish a person merely passing such a place; therefore, till one is found guilty of a crime, he cannot be fined or sent to either.
6. Whoever gets in a Passion must be taken to the Water, have a ducking to cool him and pay a fine of one.
7. Whoever gets into Idleness must come to Poverty.
8. Whoever gets into the Road to Folly must return to Prudence.
9. Whoever becomes a Liar, Swearer and Breaker of the Sabbath, must be taken to the Whipping Post and Whipt, and pay a fine of one.
10. Whoever becomes a Cheat, must be sent to Bridewell for one moth, pay a fine of one and when at liberty begin the game again.
11. Whoever becomes a Perjurer must be put in the Pillory and pay a fine of one.

12. Whoever becomes a drunkard, must be put in the stocks and pay a fine of one.
13. Whoever becomes a robber must be sent to Newgate for two months, pay a fine of two and when at liberty begin the game again.
14. Whoever arrives at the summit of dissipation, must go to ruin and pay a fine of three.
15. Whoever is confined to Bridewell or Newgate, cannot be relieved till his allotted time expires or some person guilty of the same crime is sent there.
16. When two persons come together, the last thrower must take possession of the place from whence he came and not pay one; except, first, when two come together and the last thrower is found guilty of an offence, He after having pad his fine, must take the place of the former, without paying more; the other person must advance or return (if not a cheat or robber, see rule 10 and 13) to the original place of the last thrower, and not pay any. – Secondly when two come together at Bridewell or Newgate, and one is confined for a crime; in that case as the last thrower cannot relieve the person confined, he must return to the place from whence he came and throw again, before he must remain as he was.
17. Whoever arrives at 67 The Mansion of Happiness, wins the game; but if he throws over he must begin the game again.

5 Details of the aim are given on the rules as a Brief Idea of the Game:

The idea of the game is to buy and rent or sell properties so profitably that players increase their wealth – the wealthiest becoming the eventual winner. Starting from 'GO', move the tokens around the board according to throw of the dice. When a player's token lands on a space not already owned, he may buy it from the Bank: otherwise it is auctioned off to the highest bidder. The object of owning property is to collect rents from opponents stopping there. Rentals are greatly increased by the erection of Houses and Hotels, so it is wise to build them on some of your building sites. To raise money, building sites may be mortgaged to the Bank. Community Chest and Chance cards give instructions that must be followed. Sometimes players land in jail. The game is one of shrewd and amusing trading and excitement.

Bibliography and Other Resources

A wealth of reference material is available on the Internet; however, books are still the most valuable way of finding out about games. During the nineteenth century, books were published, usually under the titles *Girl's Own* and *Boy's Own*, which included games and sports along with adventure tales and moral stories. Many of the books now available give further reading lists.

Arnold, Arnold, *The World of Children's Games* (London: MacMillan London Ltd, 1975)

Bell, R.C., *Board and Table Games from many Civilisations* (London: OUP, 1960)

Bett, Henry, *The Games of Children, Their Origins and History* (London: Methuen & Co., 1929)

Child, Mrs L. Maria, *The Girl's Own Book, 1834* (Bedford, MA, USA: Applewood Books, 1992)

Clarke, William, *The Boy's Own Book, 1829* (Bedford, MA, USA: Applewood Books, 1996)

Cooper, Rosaleen, *Games from an Edwardian Childhood* (London: David & Charles, 1982)

Daiken, Lesley, *Children's Games throughout the Year* (London: B.T. Batsford Ltd, 1949)

Gomme, Alice B., *The Traditional Games of England, Scotland and Wales* (London: Thames & Hudson, 1984)

Goodfellow, Caroline G., *A Collector's Guide to Games and Puzzles* (London: Apple Press, 1991)

Grunfeld, Frederic V., *Games of the World* (New York: Holt Rinehart & Winston, 1975)

Ickis, Marguerite, *The Book of Games and Entertainment the World Over* (New York: Dodd & Mead, 1969)

MacCuaig, D. and Clark, G.S., *Games Worth Playing* (London: Longmans, Green & Co., 1940)

Newell, William W., *Games and Songs of American Children* (New York: Dover Publications, 1963)

Opie, Iona and Peter, *Children's Games in Street and Playground* (Oxford: OUP, 1979)

Reeves, Boleyne, *Colburn's Kalendar of Amusements for 1840* (London: Henry Colburn, 1840)

Whitehill, Bruce, *American Boxed Games and their Makers* (USA: Wallace-Homestead, 1992)

Whitehouse, F.R.B., *Table Games of Georgian and Victorian Days* (Priory Press Ltd, 1971)

Other Resources

For those who are particularly interested in certain games it is possible that they may be available to play on the Internet. Games such as *Monopoly*, *Scrabble*, *Go* and *Cluedo* are available. They also have national and international tournaments.

Two major associations are associated with board games, both with websites – Board Games Studies and The American Games Collectors Association. These associations have members who conduct research into various aspects of games. Much of this research has been published.

Museums

Games are part of social development, of the single child and one within a family unit as well as within the wider community. A number of museums have games within their collections, rarely as separate displays, usually as part of wider social history displays. However, there are a few which have substantial collections suitable for research:

British Museum, London
Young V&A, London
Museum of Childhood, Edinburgh
Museum and Archive of Games, Waterloo, ON, Canada
Essex Institute, Salem, MA, USA
Strong, National Museum of Play, Rochester, NY, USA

Acknowledgements

I would like to express my grateful thanks to John Williams for his illustrations and the photographs taken of my games; to Elizabeth and Amy Hunter who excelled at showing just how games should be played; and to James Masters for his assistance and additional photographs. Likewise, thanks go to Lisa Mitchell and Joanna Howe, The History Press, for all their help and advice.

Grateful thanks are also extended to Kate Armitage, Gemma Bolton, Natalie Cahillane, John Cardy, Owen Davies, Patsy Ellis, Sandy Guthrie, Joe Jaques, Shelley Jones-Fenleigh and Jennifer Snyder and the companies that they represent for all their help and information.

And to Josephine Goodfellow for her total support and to Tango and Twizzle for their total acceptance go my thanks.

Companies Involved

Cooperman Company, www.cooperman.com
Design Master Associates Inc., www.designmasters.com
Garden Games Ltd, www.gardengames.co.uk
Gibsons Games, www.gibsonsgames.co.uk
Hasbro UK Ltd, www.hasbro.co.uk
House of Jaques, www.jaques.co.uk
Invicta Toys and Games Ltd, www.invicta-group.co.uk
Masters Traditional Games, www.mastersgames.com
(SIC) Design, www.sicdesignerservices.com

Index